Grandpa Gordon's Book of Light Hearted Poetry and Anecdotes

Grandpa Gordon's Book of Light Hearted Poetry and Anecdotes

BY GRANDPA GORDON

Grandpa Gordon's Book of Light Hearted Poetry and Anecdotes
Copyright © 2012 by Gordon Jevons

Book design by The Troy Book Makers

Printed in the United States of America

The Troy Book Makers • Troy, New York • thetroybookmakers.com

To order additional copies of this title,
contact your favorite local bookstore
or visit www.tbmbooks.com

ISBN: 978-1-61468-089-5

FOREWARD

Throughout my life I have enjoyed humor and writing simple rhyming poetry. At the suggestion of a couple of friends and some family, I decided to put some of it together in the form of a small book. There are poems, some stories, and a few anecdotes.

The main reason for pursuing this fun endeavor was to leave something that could serve as a remembrance for my grandchildren and, hopefully, a multitude of great-grandchildren.

Not to go into any amount of biographical detail, I will simply state that by growing older, through aging and knowledge, I became conservative. Some of my poems of a political nature have a conservative theme. I ask of any liberal readers to please be tolerant of my senior citizen views.

There will be further explanations of some of the writings as the pages turn.

Before moving on, I wish to thank family and friends for their encouragement and, most of all, God, for the time and ability to accomplish it.

PROLOGUE

Writing and compiling this book is something that I had long thought about doing and decided that, at this stage in my life, I had better get to it. Some of the poems and all of the anecdotes were based on events that actually took place. The poems pretty much will tell their own story, but in some cases a short paragraph of explanation will precede the poem.

~Why "Grandpa Gordon?" The fact is that, at this time, I have nineteen grandchildren and three great-grandchildren. Also, years ago, I thought that if I attempted something of this nature, I would follow the example of Anna Mary Robertson Moses. At age 75, in the nearby village of Eagle Bridge, New York, she created her first painting for public display and signed that painting as "Grandma Moses." She continued painting for many years and became famous. That is not my intent, however, and I will remain just plain "Grandpa Gordon." I want to note that all of my grandchildren are now young adults and can handle any of the words that may be a little off-color.

~My father was an orphan and the only grandparents I had were my mother's mom and dad, Anna and Henry Steurwald. They were caring, and industrious, and perfect role models of rural farm life. Being the first-born grandchild I received an abundance of love and attention. I learned much from them and they will be referenced several times in the following pages.

~There will be some poems concerning the Trapp Family Lodge and Resort located in the mountains of northern Vermont. This is where the Von Trapp family made their home after fleeing Hitler and the Nazis prior to World War II. It was the story of this courageous and musical family that inspired The Sound of Music. They chose this area of Vermont because it reminded them of their home in Austria. Over the years, the family transformed this vast mountainside property from a farm to the wonderful family resort that it is today. It has become our vacation home where we spend several weeks each year. Some of my Trapp Family poems relate to humorous events and a couple of these were dropped into the suggestion box at the Lodge.

~Dr. William Feeney is my primary care physician and he is referenced in a couple of the poems. For my reasonably healthy condition I want to credit the others on my medical team. My cardiologist, Dr. Michael Bernstein, takes very good care of my ticker. Dr. Thomas Couch, a podiatrist, works diligently to keep my feet in good shape. For some vascular issues and surgery, Dr. Kathleen Ozsvath has come to my rescue. I am indebted to and thank them all.

~Wherefore Reilly? The young ones grow up, move on and start families of their own. Then, one by one, the pets they left behind also depart. Time to tear up tainted carpets and refinish stained hardwood floors. At last a pet-free zone and the freedom from caring for pets.

Alas! One summer, a five year old granddaughter came for a visit and stayed due to a family situation, from first grade through high school and, now, into college. Immediately she wanted a pet. Minimal care was the password. Gold fish, hamsters and hermit crabs were tried. All did not succeed and it was a pet-free zone again. Tenacious, that little girl was and near the end of her high school career she came home with the news of a six month old pedigreed black lab that needed a home. Off she and grandma went and returned with Reilly. He was trained, well-behaved, and extremely intelligent Though he belonged to Lindsay, he decided to adopt the two adults in the home as his caretakers. You will read some things about Reilly.

This book has no audio counterpart. Complete this page as a vision test and you will be able to continue.

THE EYE EXAM

An American lad of Czech descent
Was a working man and a proper gent.

He noticed at times, problems with vision.
A visit to the clinic was a firm decision.

He was led to a room where he sat on a chair
To look at a chart on the wall over there.

There were rows of letters,
   both bold and fine,
Where the size grew smaller
   going down each line.

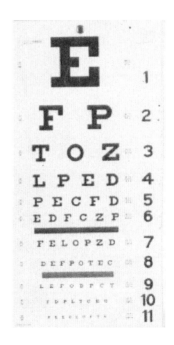

The doctor picked one
   down low on the chart,
"We'll try this line.
   It's a good one to start.

Can you read me these letters?
   What do you say?"
There was K S L O X R F B and A.

The lad looked at those symbols,
   almost a dozen.
He smiled and said, "Read it?
   That boy is my cousin!"

Lucky was I that my teen-age grandson, Sam Cowey, agreed to do illustrations for some of my poems. He has a great sense of humor and he is, in my opinion, a darn good artist. I hope you enjoy his drawings as much as I have.

Church Plaques

The young lad stood there in the church front hall,
Reading men's names on the plaques on the wall.

The curious youth was polite and well-reared.
And while standing there, the good Father appeared.

"Father, what are those names?" he asked, somewhat nervous.
"My son, those are the men that have died in the service."

"Oh, thank you, dear Father. Could you please tell me when?
Was it the eight o'clock service or was it the ten?"

Mouth Control

Once the words are spoken they can't be taken back.
Thus, staying out of trouble takes a bit of tact.
I have this good advice, that happiness will bring,
Always think about it twice and then don't say a thing!

The Golf Ball

The golfer in the clubhouse
Was admiring his little white ball.
He spouted praises about it
To the wonderment of all.

A buddy in his foresome
Asked him about that pellet.
If there is something special,
Won't you please just tell it?

"Okay my friend, I'll tell you,
It is worth whatever the cost,
This little dimpled white thing,
No way it can be lost.

If you hit it off into the rough,
After an errant swing,
It will sit there nicely hidden
And a bell will start to ring.

Or slice it down into the woods,
Behind some trees and thistle,
This little ball acts proudly
And gives a piercing whistle.

When you get a bad roll,
Into a pond or stream,
It cranks up its tiny engine
And shoots off a jet of steam."

The buddy asked where he got it,
His marvel of whistle, steam and ring,
The golfer answered "Would you believe it?
One day I found the thing!"

One Scary Night

Grandpa was a Jack-of-all-trades and known as "a man for all seasons." Among his many talents were those of a farmer, blacksmith, butcher and animal healer. Henry Steuerwald was always willing to lend a helping hand to anyone in need. He could mend a broken piece of machinery or cure an ailing cow. Got a problem? Ask Henry.

Nana, a hard worker, had her own special talents. She was an outstanding cook, homemaker, mother, and telephone operator. Yes, telephone operator! The main feature of Nana's large country kitchen was the switchboard corner. In the early days of telephone communication, the central phone company would locate branch switchboards in the smaller rural areas. Nana's board covered the village of Canaan, Queechy Lake, Berkshire Farm, and all the surrounding homes and farms. Such was the cord board in her kitchen. Party lines, multiple rings, and the board operation are for another story.

In those days, due to a known lack of privacy, phone conversations were usually short, business-like, and with minimal gossip. Late night calls were either very important or an emergency. Regular social calls were rarely made after 9 PM.

With the phone service located in my grandparents home, the fire siren to alert the volunteers was located on a tall pole about three feet from the house. If a call came in late at night, an alarm sounded in my grandparents' bedroom. Should that alarm sound, Nana would rush down to the board. If it was a fire call, she would pull the knob to activate the ear-splitting siren.

One warm August evening, after a busy day of following Grampa all over the farm and downing a man-sized supper, I settled in bed for a deep sleep. The gentle breeze through the screened window, the rustling of the leaves in the trees, and the lullaby of frequent train whistles at the numerous crossings, quickly moved me into dreamland. You guessed it! Somewhere in the middle of the night, around 2 AM, the alarm woke Nana and she promptly did her thing. A fire it was.

Can you imagine what the blasting of that siren, heard for miles in any direction and about 10 feet from my ears, did to a sound

asleep five-year-old? I'll tell you what it did. To say it scared the living be-jammers out of me would be a gross understatement. I jumped high enough to set an Olympic record and my heart raced fast enough to win the Indy 500!! And, yes, I screamed and cried up a storm. My discomfort, however, was short lived. I calmed in a matter of minutes. There is nothing quite as healing and soothing as the loving arms of a super Nana and Grampa. My scary night was over but never forgotten.

Added notes: The spontaneous combustion hay fire was quickly contained by the volunteers with slight damage. None of the farm animals were involved. You might say a satisfactory ending.

Bill Munch, a local electrician and Canaan old-timer, informed me that the siren, at the time of its purchase, was state-of-the-art and very expensive. That siren serves the community to this day. A hundred years of faithful service and, as it turns out, a real bargain.

His Last Words

The Sunday Mass had ended and empty were the pews,
When Martha approached the preacher. She had some awful news.
The good Priest greeted his child. She was disheveled in his sight,
As she related to the Father, "My husband, he died last night."

"Dear Martha that's disheartening. It is nothing I'd have guessed."
Then gently he inquired, "Did he have a last request?"
"Oh yes, he did, dear Father. And it was an urgent plea.
As the truth would have it, they were his final words to me."
"What were those pleading words, so I may help my son?"
His last request she repeated. "Martha, put down that gun!"

COINCIDENCE

He drove his wife to the dentist
To replace a fallen out filling.
She had no license to drive so
To take her he was willing.

While sitting in the waiting room
His back molar began to ache.
The pain kept growing stronger,
Soon more than he could take.

I'm here, I'll see the doctor now,
Being quick of wit and mental.
Getting that ache in the waiting room,
I call that coinci-dental!

Grandpa Steuerwald was a friend of James Otis, the inventor of the elevator.

GOOD ADVICE

Grandpa got a message from his good friend Jimmy O.
"Henry, please come over, there is something I want to show."
Grandpa hooked up the horse and buggy, on this lazy summer day,
Down the lane and onto the road, happily on his way.
Wondering what it was, curiosity without end,
You'd never know with Jimmy, his creative inventor friend.

Grandpa soon arrived at Jimmy's humble place,
Where his good friend stood proudly, a smile upon his face.
He displayed this little room that he could move from side to side.
"It goes from here to over there," he stated full of pride.
Grandpa thought intently, a wrinkle furrowed his brow.
He knew there was a purpose, he had to figure how.
Then he smiled broadly. "Jimmy, I do declare!
Make that room go up and down. You'll be a millionaire."

HOMEWORK DOG

He told the teacher the dog ate his homework,
He said it each day without fail.
Of course, she never believed him,
Until that dog graduated from Yale!!

Jose the Baseball Fan or Yankee Hospitality

In San Juan, Puerto Rico, there lived this one fine fellow.
Jose had lots of friends, he was likable and mellow.
He worked hard and saved his money. He had a worthy plan,
To go to New York City; he was a Yankee fan.
A visit to the stadium to see his heroes play,
He gathered all his savings, 'twould be a special day.
A flight to JFK, then to the Bronx he'd go.
Taxi drivers were no problem, 'cause Spanish he did know.
They drove to Yankee Stadium. It was a gorgeous day.

But the game was all sold out. He was filled with great dismay
He had a pocket full of money, yet no seats could be had.
Unfortunate is what he was, Jose became quite sad.
He told a guard his story, trembling with each word.
Derrick Jeter, as fate would have it, walked by and overheard.
The short stop with great talent, had compassion too,
He told Jose, "Don't worry, I'll see what we can do."
They sat him by the flag pole at the wall in center field.
If a ball or player came his way, he must quickly yield.
He always would remember this highlight of his life,
Before returning home to daily toil and strife.
The red-eye flight back home to his Caribbean isle,
He thought of his wondrous day with a constant smile
Next day his friends did meet him and asked if he had fun.
"Si, si" and "mucho grande," plus his beloved Yanks had won.
They asked him of the one thing that he'd remember most.
He said the players and the fans, they were the perfect host.
Before the game was started, it got quiet as could be.
Everybody stood, looked my way and sang, "Jose, can you see?

8

Way back in the thirties when electricity and radio were the greatest things in life and entertainment, youngsters pretty much had to amuse themselves. A visit to Nana and Grandpa Steuerwald's farm always made that task a lot easier, as there were many, many things to do. In the house Nana always had a multitude of tasty treats. Many hours could be spent gliding back and forth on the porch swing that hung from the ceiling. It was even fun to watch Nana operate the community telephone switchboard, located in the corner of her kitchen.

On the farm itself, there were many things to do. There were animals to visit and view. I remember the team of horses, the plow mule, the pigs and the chickens. There was the hay mow where you could swing out on a rope and drop into the soft hay below. There were trees to climb, fields to romp in, and several interesting places to play hide-and-seek. My earliest memories were of cousin Joann and me on the farm. Being the first-born grandchildren, we received an abundance of love and special treatment.

THE ROOSTER GOOSED HER

On one of those nice summer Saturdays on the farm, Joann and I were doing some of the usual things. After visiting the barn and the pig pen, and jumping in the hay mow, we decided to visit with the chickens at the chicken coop. The younger chickens were kept enclosed in a fenced-in portion of that facility. The older chickens, the laying hens, and roosters, were allowed to wander about the farm and to peck anything that, to them, seemed worthy of pecking. The adult wanderers were aware of predators and usually did not stray too far from the safety of their home.

On this particular day, as we strolled among these brightly colored leghorns, an ornery big old rooster took a dislike to us and decided, due to our age and size, to give us a chase. He came running at us with wings flailing and squawking, the most frightening sounds one would ever want to hear. Joann and I took off. Now, being just under five, I hadn't developed any hero tendencies, and being a few months older than Joann, I was able to outrun her and that bird. Unfortunately, he caught up to her and was able to peck her once on the knee and twice on the buttocks before she escaped him atop the woodpile.

Our screams, and his squawking, brought Joann's father, my Uncle Frank, running from the house. Nana treated and soothed Joann's wounds while Uncle Frank and Grandpa quickly dispatched that rooster.

After church the next day, we all sat down to Nana's wonderful, tasty Sunday dinner, featuring fresh garden vegetables and one well-done, ornery rooster. After dinner Joann and I retired to the porch swing. She sat on a cushion.

Round-a-bouts have become the latest solution to intersection traffic problems. Recently almost a dozen have been built in the area of Round Lake, New York.

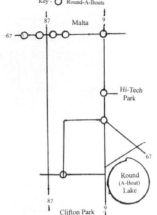

In Malta and Round Lake
they have round-a-bouts galore,
And every time I drive there,
I find they've added more.

It would be very fitting,
so this suggestion I do make,
Change the name of that body of water;
call it Round-a-bout Lake!

The workers of our local power company have a strong labor union. Linemen only run lines. Pole men only erect poles. Meter men only install meters. These different crews wait their turn while all the time on the clock.

Unionized

The temporary work crew was taken to the job,
And told to wait instructions from Supervisor Bob.

"This is quite embarrassing," said one of the workers, named Sid.
"Standing here doing nothing, they'll think we're National Grid."

A common form of humor is the put-down joke. This is usually the style in a celebrity roast. In years past, Polish and Irish people were the butt of this humor. In these times, it is lawyers and ladies with blond hair that are the recipients. There will be some of these on the following pages. Most of the beautiful blond ladies I know are good sports, fully understand that it is humor, and laugh along. For those that are offended, I apologize. As for lawyers? Well, that is entirely different.

WORD WORK

A blonde secretary was hired for a job to fill,
But lacked word processing and computer skill.
Let me explain, so you'll know what I mean,
She put white-out all over the monitor's screen!

Most colleges require their student athletes to maintain passing grades in all subjects. Players with high academic scores are honored as scholar athletes. The NCAA has rules requiring players to be in good academic standing. Some schools, however, have a great interest in winning and oft times fudge the scores.

A Real Scholar?

There was a college athlete whose grades were in contention.
He had missed many contests due to academic suspension.

Once cleared to play again, he returned to the game.
And the reporters all were curious about this player's fame.
They asked the team's head coach how well he was performing.
"He is now our new team leader and our record he's reforming."

"What about all his studies? How is he doing these days?"
"He's working diligently and he's making all straight As."
The reporters were impressed. They took his words for granted.
Until the coach added, "But his Bs are a little slanted."

Language

Many years ago I taught a fifth grade class in a suburban district outside the city of Albany. It was a K-6 school with two classes of each grade. Each class enrolled between twenty and thirty students.

One day in the middle of the fall semester a family, newly arrived from Italy, brought a fourth grade aged boy to enter the school. Little Vinnie spoke almost no English. Sadly, no one in the teaching or custodial staff spoke or understood Italian. It was suggested that, perhaps, one of the 5th or 6th grade students possibly spoke Italian. Inquiring, we found Chuck, a sixth grader who assured us that he spoke the tongue of Italy.

Proceeding to the library where Vinnie was waiting, Chuck asked us what he should say to start the conversation. We all agreed that Chuck should ask Vinnie his name. Thus, Chuck walked over to the waiting lad and, with a big smile on his face, Chuckie leaned over and said "Ay, keed, watts ah you name?" As they say, even the best laid plans of mice and men...

With the aid of a couple of English/Italian dictionaries and an eager little Italian lad, the entire school was having fun. The American students learned a few words in Italian, and little Vinnie was becoming quite fluent in English.

It is to be noted that our little hero successfully completed elementary school. He was an honor student throughout high school and a running star on the cross-country team.

I must sadly admit that, after he entered college, I lost track of Vinnie. But, knowing his drive and determination, I'm sure he had a successful career and life.

I get a strange thought every now and then
Like, "Right now, I'm the oldest I've ever been."

Postal workers retire and now there is this quip.
"Mailmen never die. They just lose their zip."

As I was approaching my seventy-fifth birthday, and growing older, I decided that I would write a short poem to commemorate each of my ensuing September 25th special days. Starting with seventy-nine and feeling fine:

~~79~~

When young, my eyes were hearty and hale.
Then, growing older, they begin to fail.
It is not too bad, and I am not too sad.
I've learned to make love by Braille.

The Sound of English

American English, as a language, to me sometimes astounds,
When a word that is spelled one way can have two different sounds.
To me, as a young scholar, it was something to dread.
Was it a book to **Read,** or had it already been **Read**?"
And when a homonym appears upon the scene;
Same pronunciation, but what exactly does it mean?
My licorice clarinet has a bamboo **Reed.**
To play musical notes on the scale that I **Read.**
I played a melodic score from a book covered in **Red.**
And made great mellow sounds from the notes that I had **Read.**

I'm stopping here now 'cause my **Allowed** time is shrinking.
This is exactly what happens, when **Aloud** I've been thinking.

On Your Toes

While away on vacation, one clear summer day,
The boy went with his parents to see the ballet.
He watched all the dancers, wondering why they chose
To do most of the movements on the tips of their toes.
He witnessed the jumps and the twists and the twirls,
And asked, "Why didn't they just get taller girls?"

And Vats That

Safety in the workplace is a most desired thing.
Yet accidents do happen, and tragedy they bring.
Sue's husband worked in the brewery where Guinness beer was made.
He was a happy man and he truly enjoyed his trade.
One day while at her stove, there was knocking on her door.
There stood her husband's co-worker. "What's wrong?" she did implore.
"Your husband, he did drown, by falling into a Guinness vat."
"Oh my God!" she did reply. "There could be nothing worse that that!"
He attempted to console her. Could he help? He wanted to know.
She asked if her man did suffer, or if quickly did he go?
"No, he didn't go quickly, and that's what puzzles me...
That ornery husband of yours climbed out three times to pee."

~~80~~

Two weeks before my birthday, I had a wonderful surprise.
I attended a college luncheon and couldn't believe my eyes.
There sat all my family, my friends, and cousins too.
To help celebrate my birthday. I was shocked, that's true.
There was no college luncheon. That was just a ruse
To get me to the function. They needed an excuse.
It was a real fine party, and with the help of the Almighty,
Perhaps I'll be duped again when approaching the age of ninety.

An important part of enjoying a polo match is having good food and beverages to enhance the experience. Several years ago, my favorite polo beverage was Heineken beer. On two consecutive evenings, the polo club was out of that brand. The next scheduled event was the Saratoga Polo celebration of the famed Travers Stakes Race. An exotic lobster dinner was planned for that special polo evening. I was promised that plenty of Heineken would be on the scene. This poem was published in the Saratoga Polo Magazine. It also helped encourage the Heineken distributorship to become a polo sponsor.

Out Again of Heineken

Off to the polo for a night of fun.
To follow the action, and watch the ponies run.
The field was firm and the sky was clear,
Anticipating the evening with people of cheer.

Our table was ready and Ryan stood by,
Fluer waved to us and Jim Rossi said, "Hi!"
We quickly sat down with a scoresheet in hand,
As the thought of a cool brew made me feel grand.

We'll have one Pinot Noir and a Heineken too,
But Ryan said, "Sorry, I no can do.
We have Amstel and Coors, both of them lite.
And one called Corona. That's all at this site."

I felt like an angus on its way to the slaughter,
Being offered a bottle of half beer and half water.
Jeanne had her Pinot before the anthem was played,
And Ryan retuned from wherever he'd strayed.
He said, "There is O.J. and vodka galore.
How about a screwdriver and perhaps a few more?"

I accepted his choice and his promise true,
That when I came back, they would have my brew.
I'm looking forward to this Travers night well-planned,
With a lobster on my plate and a Heineken in my hand!

TIMELY

Roofer Murphy, one day, was as busy as could be.
Fixing a church roof, in the village of Tralee.
He grew curious with wonder when the church tower would chime.
And decided his own watch would tell him the time.
He reached for the timepiece, up under his sleeve,
When it fell from his hand and rolled down off the eave.
He ran to the ladder and hustled downward bound!
Catching that Timex before it hit the ground!
How could that have happened? Viewers wanted to know.
"Because," he smiled, "that watch is always five minutes slow!"

Brandished

Three successful CEOs worked and lived in the city strife.
One day these friends grew tired of that New York City life.
They knew a change was needed, a change to better their lot.
A place to work and live, in an uncrowded country spot.
They talked about a cattle ranch out in western prairie spaces.
The thought of a fresh air lifestyle put smiles upon their faces.
For Sale: A spread in Wyoming, of over one thousand acres,
It was that our three good partners bought. Oh yes, they were the takers.
They worked a serious plan, and their city holdings did divest.
Packed up, said their farewells, and diligently headed west.
Their endeavor would be equal, each with a one-third share.

They'd respect one another and always keep it fair.
A new name now was needed for the cattle ranch they bought,
That each could have his own choice, and they all agreed on that thought.

A few months went by and a city friend had business in the west,
Planning a visit to his old pals, and he would be their guest.
They greeted him with open arms. He was awed by the space and views.
Old friends chatting and laughing, getting caught up on all the news.
There, sitting on the veranda, while the sun was setting red,
He inquired of the partners, "What did you name this spread?"
They informed him each one had a say, all three had a chance.
The Partners Three, Shining Moon, River Bend, Prairie Grass,
      Western Wind, Cattle Ranch.
"I haven't seen your herd out there.
      Where are they standing?"
"We started with five hundred,
      but none survived the branding!"

Law is a highly respected profession. One must go through many strenuous years of studies to earn a law degree, and then pass the bar exam to become licensed. I have met and have known many great lawyers in my lifetime. However, as in all groups, there are good ones and bad ones. And, in that same lifetime, I have known some really bad ones. Here is how these bad ones deal with their clients

    The attorney rules for handling a client.
    Be forceful and stern and always defiant.
    Greet them aloofly, then face them and seat them,
    Contemplating the numerous ways you can cheat them.

If they come in upset and are extremely worried,
Never, ever, allow yourself to be hurried.
When the client is thinking that all may be lost,
Simply inform them of the tremendous cost.
Smile, shake their hand, with a confident face.
And brag that only you can handle their case.
Become unavailable to the point of a laugh.
Every time that they call, they speak only to staff.
The final rule, after you've employed every antic.
Don't return their call until they're completely frantic!

Crooks & Politicians

Throughout the world under darkness not sun,
Crooks steal the money and away they run.
Here in America, whether it is dark or it's sunny,
Politicians run and then they take the money!!

Often, travel by air presents problems such as delays, cancellations, lost luggage and missed connections. A few years ago I had a weekend round-trip journey, in which all of these could have occurred, but they didn't. Thus, I wrote a tribute to the carrier.

To—U.S. Airways
    Subject- Roundtrip Albany to Key West
    Two senior citizens- one adult

On April 4, 2008 we had an early flight to Key West via Washington and Ft. Lauderdale. I have a leg problem, and was courteously provided with wheel-chair assistance at all points. The trip was on-time and without problem.

Our late afternoon return trip on Sunday, April 6, could have been a relative disaster. There was a huge amount of congestion at the small Key West terminal and connecting locations in Florida

19

were experiencing severe weather conditions. Late take-offs, missed connections, and whole day delays were experienced by passengers on other carriers.

The care, concern, and assistance of the U.S. Airways personnel and the relative success of our journey prompted me to write the following poem.

Thank you U.S. Air
    Flight numbers: April 4–771 and 3849
        April 6–4062, 1940 and 1947

U.S. Air is Good for You

When visiting Florida, to a place called Key West,
Fly U.S. Airways. They are the very best!
To Washington and Lauderdale, then to Key West you see,
U.S. Air flew us there–like one, two, three.
They took great care, we had nothing to do.
We arrived quickly and safely. Our luggage did too.
A pleasant Key visit, then we had to return.
There was congestion and bad weather, we soon did learn.
Despite the confusion and bustle, they eased us aboard
Finally an O.K. from Orlando–wheels up, we roared.
Our pilot held steady, he knew just what to do
This small regional jet had a fabulous crew.
In the dark quirky skies, with explosions and lulls,
With seat belts fastened we protected our skulls.
A very fine landing, true and straight,
Then taxi-ing the plane to the designated gate.
The terminal staff and the crew from the plane
Umbrella'd our heads because of the rain.
For our Charlotte connection, so we wouldn't be late
They wheel-chaired me right over to the proper gate.

Soon, comfortably seated in twenty-three A
The captain announced that there would be a delay

We needed more fuel. That's not a bit frightening.
But they can't do the job when there's thunder and lightening.
We amused ourselves for fifty minutes or so,
Then the engines roared and away we did go,
To Carolina and Charlotte for our final leg.
Get us there on time, I did pray and beg.
They pushed it along, that great U.S. Air,
And landed in Charlotte, with only minutes to spare.

We arrived at the far end of the concourse D,
Our Albany plane was way out on concourse C.
A U.S. Air lady said that we must hurry,
Another grabbed my chair, and away we did scurry.
She radioed ahead and then hunkered down.
There is no doubt; she could win the Triple Crown.
The other two running, and my pusher in stride,
Across the main terminal to a concourse ride.
Beeping and twisting, with moves galore,
Our driver took us to the jet-way door.
They were waiting and took me and turned me around.
In a matter of minutes, we were Albany bound.

A most comfortable flight, serene and sublime,
Through the night. We arrived ahead of time.
At the start of the day, a bag we had checked.
It also made changes. It was not direct.
Imagine how greatly relieved we felt
When our bag came out riding on the moving belt.
The best part of this story, I want to relate:
U.S. Air personnel, they really are great!
Meeting your needs with courtesy and care.
Most important of all, they get you there.

Kudos to U.S. Airways, amazing you are!
Fly U.S. Air
They are the best by far!

Kevin Mullen, the President of Siena College, is an ardent follower of the Siena Saints basketball team. It is well known that, on occasion, he will seek divine assistance for the teams success.

How Father Kevin Won the Game
For the Siena Basketball Saints

Father Kevin is humble, yet he has no restraints
When asking God's help for a win by his Saints.
In Springfield City that has The Hall of Fame,
The team was there for the first round game.
The Jaspers from Manhattan is the team they would meet,
And for Siena, an opening win would really be sweet.
Both teams played well and both were in it,
As the clock ran down to under a minute.
Manhattan's last shot would give them the win,
If the flight path was true and the ball went in.
The Siena fans jumped up and gave a shout.
As the ball spun 'round the rim and finally rolled out,
Father Kevin glanced upward. His head gave a nod,
And he humbly said, "Thank you, oh thank you, God."

Siena lost the next round. The end for the Saints.
But the fans and the players have no complaints.
Injuries and issues left not much to cheer.
But, as they once said in Brooklyn, "Wait till next year."
The Saints will be strong. The best of the best.
And Father Kevin and God will have a well-earned rest.

A Divine Scolding

Two enterprising young lads were seeking some work to do.
They formed a painting company, titled "We will paint for you."
A special job was their desire, to get the business started.
They discovered a little church where the siding and paint had parted.
Off they went to the pastor, to make a contract deal,

And offered him a low price that they knew would appeal.
There was agreement on the cost, with a handshake and a blessing.
But how to pay for all those buckets had the two boys guessing.
They had the cash on hand to buy half the buckets they would need,
So they would stretch the paint adding water. A bad idea, indeed!
Painting began in the morning and they worked the whole day through,
To finish by noon the next day, well after the morning dew.
The church, like new, it glistened there under the sunlit sky.
The Pastor warmly grinned with a shining smile in each eye.
All of a sudden the blue sky darkened, and a cloudburst spoiled the day,
As a torrential deluge of rainfall washed the weakened paint away.
Then a voice roared down from the Heavens. "That is something I abhor!
And the Lord advised those brushmen: "Repaint, and thin no more!"

MIXED UP,

He was an insomniac	At night time in slumber
With an agnostic view.	Couldn't sleep like a log.
And another problem,	Laid awake all in wonder,
He was dyslexic too.	Was there really a dog?

After many, many years of no post season success, the Boston Red Sox of late have become play-off and World Series winners. Through the summer months of 2011, they were almost assured of at least a wild card spot. However, the wheels came off the train in September and they lost their chance in the final inning of the final regular season game. Alas...

It defies all logic, it defies all reason,
The fat lady has sung. Fenway is closed for the season.

Bruce Saves The Day

The mid-winter ball at Shaker High School was scheduled for Saturday night. Students and sponsors worked diligently Friday after school and into the evening to make all the preparations and do the decorating for the big event. Everything was moving smoothly and on schedule until the wee hours of Saturday morning when the snow began to fall. And fall it did... Several inches every hour, all day long.

The powers that be wisely postponed the big dance until Monday night. The decorations were in place, the gowns were ready, and the corsages had been purchased. It was the logical night for the ball.

I was working in the outer office of the Senior Hall principal that Monday morning when a problem developed. Many of the young ladies had scheduled appointments at beauty salons that were canceled on that snowy Saturday, and it is a known fact that beauty parlors and salons are closed on Mondays. Many of the young ladies needed those appointments.

I have a friend who owned and operated Bruce's Glamour Chalet, not too far from the school. It was worth the try, so I gave him a call. Bruce is a kind and caring man and he agreed to open the shop that day for the girls. A grim situation soon turned into a happy one. With the cooperation of the principal, the school, and the approval of the parents, a hair disaster became a thing of beauty. Bruce worked his magic on almost thirty young ladies that day and helped make that mid-winter ball a most memorable success.

Echoing the words of those many young ladies, I want to repeat it here. Thank you, Bruce!

San Francisco Surprise

Several years ago I had a business convention date,
In the city of San Francisco, above the Golden Gate.
My historic hotel sat majestic, there atop the hill.
The cable car ride to get there, a very exciting thrill,

The hotel had been re-furbished, the fixtures all were new.
And out of the spacious window, a most fantastic view.
I unpacked and had a shower, started relaxing with ease,
Then decided on some verses, which myself would please.
I opened the Bible drawer, then jumped back with a frightful start.
Instead of a hardcover Gideon, there was Tony Bennett's heart.

Mistaken Identity

George hopped upon the subway train down in New York City.
He was a charming man, clever, and somewhat witty.

Another man came into the car, he was proper and discreet.
Being courteous, he asked, "Do you mind if I share your seat?"

"Sit right down," said George. "May I ask a question, please?
Didn't we meet once before, in the city of Los Angeles?"

"I've never been that far out west," replied the man, wonder in his eyes.
"Neither have I," said George. "It must have been two other guys!"

In my early forties, I began having problems controlling my weight. For a time, I was sixty pounds too heavy... Obese!! That led to health problems and a struggle began. It was far from easy, but now, though still slightly heavy, things are under control. I try to make good food choices, practice moderation and use some of the new dietary products that have been developed. It is much easier now and there are no more excuses.

Weight A Minute

A large foursome came into the lounge last night.
They truly qualified as an awesome sight.
In attempting to state and to cleverly define,
They were larger than the Patriots offensive line.
Judging the size of each, going one by one,
The calculation came to over half a ton!
Directed toward the windows and the chair table booth,
I have to relate something that is the total truth.
They sidled in, pulled out chairs, and when all sat down,
My walker on wheels started rolling toward town!

Fewer Government Workers

Our governments have grown too large.
Far above their original creation.
It is true throughout all of the spectrum,
In the local, the state, and the nation.
Enormity leads to more taxes,
Because of the over spending.
Increasing the public work force
Has got to come to an ending.
The largest expense is the payroll,
Started with noble intentions.
But the wages are far above average,
As well as retirement pensions.
We must reduce this work force,
As quickly as we can. For the highway workers alone
I have a strategic plan.
Get rid of the un-needed non-workers,
Retired or laid off on the shelf.
We need only to invent a good shovel
That can simply standup by itself!

A news item that received a great deal of attention involved a father-son pair of burglars. In the middle of the night, they stole large headstones from a roadside monument company. Many wondered why take such a risk for a product that would be difficult to sell. Some suggested that it was a dim-wit caper.

Great Thinkers?

Two burglars stealing headstones
In the middle of the night,
Hoping that the darkness
Would hide each one from sight.

The foolishness of this caper
Is what really astounds.
Stealing polished granite rocks
Weighing several hundred pounds.

Robbing such an item
To no one made much sense.
A monument of that size
Is impossible to fence.

All the people that should know
Thought the whole thing quite inane.
And that the father-son perps
Were most probably insane.

They answered, "We're not dummies,
We are surely two great thinkers.
We wuz goin' out whale fishin'
And needed some big sinkers!"

Justin is a long term employee working in the lounge at the Trapp family Lodge. One of the features of his fine home in rural Vermont was a stately apple tree that adorned his front yard. One autumn evening, a heavy freak snowstorm hit the area. The leaves were still on the trees and the weight of the snow split Justin's poor apple tree in half. The next evening in the lounge, Justin was not a happy camper.

Justin Had a Tree

He works at the Lodge with great dedication,
filling the needs of each person's libation.
His home's on six acres of pristine Vermont,
with his family, nothing more did he want.
The heart of his pride was a fine apple tree,
in the front of his house for all to see.

The season was Fall, but the leaves they did not,
and a wet heavy snow fell right on his spot.
The leaves became loaded, the branches did bend,
bringing his tree to it's terrible end.
One half split north and the other south bound,
And there, in the morning, it lay on the ground.

When asked how he felt when his apple tree split,
He said, "To be honest, I feel like s--t."

When bad things happen, there is often some good.
Justin now has a pile of great firewood.

Dr. Ward Stone, a prominent New York State pathologist, was asked by residents down-wind from a large capacity cement plant to investigate the area for chemical contaminants. This poem popped into my head. I didn't planet.

Mercury Gets Stoned

Pathologist Stone, one of the best in the nation,
Was commissioned to do an investigation,

By the good citizens of Coeymans Town.
Ward quickly agreed and headed on down,

To test flora and fauna, water, soil and air,
And discover what contaminants resided there.

High mercury levels, above normal, he found,
In living creatures, air, water, and ground.

I have a question, Dr. Stone, for what it is worth:
Looking deeper, would you find traces of Venus and Earth?

I wrote this poem for my mother's 95th birthday. It was read on each of her successive birthdays with an adjustment to the numbers. Along with her lifetime duties as a mother and homemaker, she played a prominent role in three different family businesses. First a neighborhood convenience store, then a busy restaurant and, finally, a harness horse breeding and training farm. Of all, she found her greatest joy in the role of grandmother. Nana passed away at the age of 105.

THE HAPPY BIRTHDAY HISTORY OF
A LADY WITH MANY TITLES, WITH MANY NAMES

Happy Birthday to YOU, Happy Birthday to YOU!
Now YOU is a good name, but here it won't do.
HAZEL LEORA STREURWALD she was christened that day;

100 years ago, she started on her way.
Endeared were her names and the titles she earned,
Now relax and listen, there's much to be learned.
Let's start with BABY, and later called DAUGHTER,
Or FARMHAND - 'go feed the chickens and carry the water.'
In school it was CLASSMATE or MY BEST FRIEND,
Or HELPER, BUDDY and PAL, yet it does not end.
She became WIFE, HELPMATE, and MOTHER to a family of four.
Formally, MRS. JEVONS, names and titles - yes there are more.
Her energy abounded, she was so active and hearty.
No wonder they called her the LIFE OF THE PARTY.
HOUSEWIFE and HOMEMAKER, when she moved to the city.
And the title STOREKEEPER - yet, she felt no pity.
Three years later a tavern, so put these on the list:
COOK, WAITRESS, DISHWASHER, I would have been (beep).
They called her HORSEWOMAN when she moved to the farm.
She worked all her titles, and still kept her charm.
Then surely it happened - events do take place,
She stated hearing NANA from many a face.
That started in the fifties - yes, way back then,
And soon she heard NANA from as many as ten.
She should have bought locks and bolted the door,
'Cause now she hears NANA from twenty-six more!
To regress a little, there were SISTER AND SIS,
Which leads us to AUNTIE - this we can't miss.
And SISTER-IN-LAW is also another,
As well as the very formal, of course, GRANDMOTHER!
In ending I'm willing to bet she likes best
The loving word NANA, of all the rest.
Take the names and the titles, all the above,
From her birth to this day, her real name is LOVE!!
HAPPY BIRTHDAY

Dog-Gone Good Sleep

At times I had trouble sleeping and didn't know what to do.
It wasn't quite insomnia, but my sleep was not always true.
My faithful good dog, Reilly, sleeps anytime, in any place.
He'll drop right off in slumber with a smile upon his face.

I needed to find his secret and I watched him for a clue,
If I could have that secret, I would know just what to do.
It didn't take me long; now I'm sleeping like a top.
I simply turn around three times and I gently flop!

Many years ago Johannes Von Trapp planted Mugho pine trees along a large stretch of Trapp Hill Road. Those trees flourished, grew tall and, unfortunately, blocked the view of the mountains from the lodge dining room. It is true that they blocked the view of the parking lot, served as a noise barrier, and held a multitude of holiday lights. The suggestion of removing them was delicate because Johannes himself had planted them. I thought that, maybe, a poetic request would help.

A Poetic Suggestion from the
Trapp Family Lodge Dining Room

While sitting at breakfast I realized some news,
behind the Mugho pines, there were mountain views.

Trouble was that the scene was blocked,
others like me were equally shocked.

Now it wouldn't take magic, or clever tricks.
This situation would be easy to fix.

Relocate those Mughos at the edge o'er the wall
and plant a hedgerow, trimmed to four feet tall.

With some arborvitaes or some shapeable yews,
that quickly would restore the Worcester Range views.

Thus properly trimmed, here is what you have got:
Real scenic beauty, and a hidden parking lot.

Such type of flora is a landscaper's dream,
'Cause it also serves as a sound barrier supreme.

This solid greenery would enhance the sights
And make perfect hanging for the Christmas lights.

Then sitting here happy, what more could you want,
With a fantastic meal, while looking at Vermont.

WENTWORTH BY-THE- SEA

My partner and I went to visit our dear friend Marion Russell in Salem, Massachusetts. The next day we decided to have lunch at her favorite place up the coast in New Hampshire. This poem tells the story.

All of us are happy, as happy as can be.
We are going for lunch at Wentworth, Wentworth-By-The-Sea.

We left our home in New York on a sunny afternoon,
A pleasant ride on the turnpike, we'd be in Salem soon.

To visit Marion Russell, a very dear, dear friend,
Waiting at the Hawthorne, at our journey's end.

She told us of a special treat on tomorrow day,
Going for lunch in New Castle, not very far away.

I asked, "Where are you taking us?" Inquisitive I be!
She replied, "We're going to Wentworth, Wentworth-by-the-Sea."

We left about mid-morning on a picture perfect day,
Passing through a lot of towns along old Route 1A.

There's Wenham, Ipswich, Hampton, Boar's Head and Newbury.
All on the way to Wentworth, Wentworth-by-the-Sea.

We saw all the scenic beauty. We savored every view,
Thinking of fine dining at a place that, to us, was new.

You go north on Route 1A, take a right on Route IB,
Drive right past the golf course, to Wentworth-by-the-Sea.

You'll see it on the skyline. It isn't very far.
Drive up to the entrance, the valet will park your car.

They'll greet you at the front door of this historic place.
The staff is there to help you with a smile on every face.

A lovely hostess seated us. We chose the porch outside.
She was extremely pleasant and she did her job with pride.

We three sat there in wonder of this very awesome setting,
Without a thought or clue of what we'd soon be getting.

I saw this vision coming, elegant, cute, and grand.
It was our server, Cheryl, I reached out to shake her hand.

She helped us with the menu, Marion, Jeanne, and me,
And started our dining pleasure at Wentworth-by-the-Sea.

There are no words to tell you of this outstanding fare.
You have to do it first-hand, yourself, you must go there.

Do yourself a favor and fill your hearts with glee.
Take all your friends to Wentworth, Wentworth-by-the-Sea.

Cheryl and the serving team treated us quite grand.
It made me think of heaven, and of the promised land.

I'm going to make a schedule and work a proper plan,
To take us back to Wentworth as often as we can.

Cheryl let me take her picture. I said, "Oh my, oh me."
I found a love in Wentworth, Wentworth- by- the- Sea.

To all of you at Wentworth,
until we meet again,
May the Good Lord bless
and keep you.
Thank you and Amen.

Dog Training

Our friendly black lab, Reilly,
    does something that is grand.
Drop something on the floor
    and he'll put it in your hand.

Early in the morning
    he does this special caper,
Running out the door and
    bringing in the morning paper.

Gently in his mouth,
    this wonderful canine chap,
Will bring it to the table
    and drop it in your lap.

Another of his talents,
    I have to tell this tale:
Write a note to someone.
    He'll deliver in-house mail.

Another special ability,
    could be considered pelf.
Our happy animal buddy does
    some training by himself.

With the mistress of the house,
    he accomplished something neat.
Sitting erect upon his haunches,
    trained her to give him a treat!

My Observation of the
Trapp Family Lodge Leaf-Peeper Season

It is in the autumn of the year.
The air is clean, and crisp, and new.
They come here by the bus loads,
To admire the foliage view.
Pretty senior ladies, enjoying
The Lodge most nights,
After the all day long touring
Of the mountain and valley sights.

They freshen in their rooms,
And quickly dress for dinner,
In that famous dining room
That is a gourmet winner.
Then gather in the lounge
To enjoy a drink or two.
Keeping time with John's piano,
With the tapping of a shoe.

I observe them all so happy,
With no cares and with no strife.
Though somewhat older and slower,
They are greatly enjoying life.

I have only one lament,
Leaving me with some grieves:
How come gorgeous,
    vibrant college girls
Don't like to look at leaves?

38

It's Reilly's Nose That Knows

Where's the morning paper,
        thrown from the passing car?
Is it somewhere near the door,
        or maybe a little far?
It could be on the porch,
        or in the flower rows.
Reilly will bring it to us.
        It's Reilly's nose that knows.

Where is the peanut butter kong?
Now just where do you suppose?
At the proper time he'll have it.
It's Reilly's nose that knows.

Where will he take care of business,
Out there where the green grass grows?
He'll find the spot for his relief.
It's Reilly's nose that knows.

What kind of storm will be coming,
From where the old west wind blows?
I can tell you it's a big one.
It's Reilly's nose that knows.

Where is the toy he had last night,
The one that Lindsay throws?
Reilly will find it quickly.
It's Reilly's nose that knows.

Who are those people walking toward us?
Are they friends or are they foes?
Reilly starts to wag his big black tail,
But it's Reilly's nose that knows.

Jimmy Casey became the owner of the historic Manor Inn in Rensselaer, NY. He changed the name to Casey's Restaurant and does a great business, with fantastic food and a friendly atmosphere. Jimmy is a rabid Yankee baseball fan and takes a great deal of ribbing from many of his Red Sox fan customers. To add to his consternation, I wrote the following:

Plan for a Bigger and Better Business

As a baby, your bottom had many a change.
So, another change now would not be strange.
But not on your bottom this time, instead,
You'll make the change up there in your head.
Forget the Bronx team and all its past glory,
Leave the Yankees like your friend, Joe Torre.
Once again be a winner and fulfill your dream,
Become a staunch fan of that great Boston team.
Put a dish on your roof. That is what you should do.
View all the Sox games, plus the Celts and Pats too.
Jimmy Casey's would become an area sensation,
As the regional home of the Red Sox nation,
Your establishment would become an outstanding winner,
As people swarm there for games, lunch and dinner!

Added note: Casey's (formerly the Manor Inn) was purchased by my parents in 1946. Under their ownership it became the weekly home of the Rensselaer Kiwanis Club, as well as the site of many weddings, parties, and special occasions. Under my father's leadership, and with the members of Kiwanis, the idea for the Rensselaer Boys Club was born. The teenage Bee Hive Canteen also became a reality at the Manor Inn. An added joy of the establishment was that it was the so-called watering hole and place of relaxation for many of the railroad workers who ran the trains from Rensselaer railroad yards and round house. My parents, Hazel and Frank Jevons (Nana and Poppy to my children,) sold the business in 1956 and moved on to own and operate the Colonie Acres harness horse farm, where they eventually retired and spent their remaining years. I was extremely proud of the way they ran the Manor Inn, making it the finest restaurant in the city. I am also proud of the way Jimmy Casey has turned it into one of the finest dining establishments in the entire Capitol Region, in spite of the fact that he is a Yankee fan.

Casey's Restaurant (Formerly the Manor Inn)

Some Manor Inn History

Back in the nineteenth century, a farmer in the foothills of Rensselaer County would spend the day gathering his crops and loading his wagon. This would start in mid-summer when the plants were in production. Before sun-up the following morning, he would hitch the team to the wagon and begin his journey to the city of Albany.

The farmer would arrive before mid-morning in the city and market his produce throughout the day. He would also purchase supplies that were needed back at the farm. At day's end he would ferry across the river to Rensselaer and proceed up Broadway to the Washington Avenue hill. Atop the hill stood the Manor Inn. Alongside and behind the Inn was a livery and stable. Here the wagon would be sheltered and the horse team stabled, fed, and watered for the night.

The farmer then would proceed to the Inn for a meal, and perhaps some libation, before taking a room for the night. This was, most likely, his only relaxation time in the entire week. Early the following morning he would again hitch the team to the wagon and journey back to the farm. This scenario would continue week after week until the end of harvest in the fall. The Manor Inn was important to the many farmers of the area for many years and an important part of history.

A Busy Night in the Trapp Family Lounge

It started off slowly, and then came the crowd.
The Lounge that was quiet, became suddenly loud.

They came for the music, to drink and to eat.
Justin had the bar, the floor had only Pete.

They rose to the challenge, this crew of two
Then along came Becky to help, she is true

John kicked up the tempo with his style and grace.
That helped our three heroes to pick up the pace.

Justifiable Justin knew just what to do,
Quickly mixing the drinks and pouring the brew.

Our waiter sweet Pete, who lives up the street,
Hustled the tables while remaining discreet.

Justin on the bar and running full throttle,
Would appear at a table to uncork a bottle.

Becky played hostess, and each one she did greet
And very efficiently found them a seat.

From Lounge to the kitchen, Pete scurried for all,
Avoiding collisions while crossing the hall.

The three worked swiftly, never seeming to tire,
With each finding time to toss a log on the fire.

Hans came along and pitched right in, what a keeper,
He even found time to maneuver the sweeper.

They served and they bussed, all through the night,
Making sure it was all done just right.

These fantastic souls make the Von Trapp a treasure,
And made our first night a wonderful pleasure.

In our country's political history, many cities were under what was called boss rule. Powerful machines of one party controlled their turf for years and years. Such was the case with the Dan O'Connell team in the city of Albany, N.Y., with Erastus Corning as mayor. One of the ways to retain their power was to control the ballot box. A loyal voter was always rewarded with a cash stipend and often voted in other wards under different names. In my retirement years, I served as an elections inspector, and am able to report that this no longer occurs.

Modern Voting

The ballot box and lever machines
    are voting things of the past.
The electronic days are with us
    and digital at last.
Carefully mark your ballot,
    and into the scanner it goes.
How you vote is kept a secret.
    It is only the machine that knows.

The polls do open early
    and go 'til nine o'clock.
When the final voter has voted
    the machine goes into lock.
The totals are immediate.
    The tally tape rolls out.
The losers, they are saddened,
    the winners cheer and shout.
All day I watched the ballots slide
    in and out of sight.

The screen quickly said 'accepted'.
    The voter had done it right.
While sitting there doing my duties,
    nostalgia came my way.
"What if we had these great machines
    in Mayor Corning's day?"
The savvy Albany voter would
    slide his filled-out ballot in,
And if he voted properly,
    the machine would kick back a fin!

After serving in the US Navy, Bill Edwardsen became a radio host and DJ. He spent almost all of his career in the Albany area. His early morning program was titled "Breakfast with Bill," and featured music of the big bands and vocalists of the thirties and forties. Bill was witty and clever. With his entertaining patter, he could lead into a commercial or song title with amazing ease. His career extended from the mid-forties through the turn of the century. Later in life, he met  and married Dr. Jean Stern, a professor from Siena College. Together they shared a passion for good music and gourmet dining. Bill's other passion was the game of golf. Upon his passing, I put these thoughts in verse for his memorial service.

Bill

A simple little verse that was written years ago,
Helps to define the man that we were proud to know.
Father called him William,
Mother called him Will,
Sister called him Willy,
But the fellas called him Bill.
The fellas were musicians, clients, friends and pals,
Listeners, and co-workers, and all the guys and gals.

He loved his kind of music. It became his life's endeavor.
And his career in radio, witty was he, and clever.
The performers and the standards were of his expertise,
He knew what people wanted and he knew just how to please.
"Breakfast with Bill," the title, it was of his own creation,
And it followed us through the decades of our aging generation.
On the music of our era, he was truly a connoisseur,
And he knew just what would please us of that you can be sure.

Some angel looking out for him, gave him Dr. Jean,
She polished up his image and improved his every scene.
Now he's gone before us, rubbing elbows with the winners,
Walking with his heroes, and eating gourmet dinners.
Plus golfing all the courses in that celestial place,
Scoring birds and eagles, and occasionally an ace.

Bill will never be forgotten, the music and the man.
A simple little ritual, a simple little plan.
When you're listening to a CD and you have a drink in hand,
Just raise a toast to William. That surely would be grand.

Myself, on many mornings, it is often that I will
Cue up his lasting music and have breakfast with our Bill.

Poker Playing Dog

My dog, Reilly, loves to play poker.
It's his favorite card table game.
He's learned face card and number values,
All about suits and cards that are the same.

He knows all about things like full houses,
And about the rules and all other stuff.
But he will never, ever, win the big pot,
Because he just doesn't know how to bluff.

If he holds the cards to be the winner,
That is when he surely will fail.
Because when he has that good hand,
He always wags his tail!

It was a normal, mud season, Saturday night in the lounge at the Trapp family lodge. Justin, David, and Henry, were on duty covering the bar, the tables, and the dining room service window. John Cassell, at the piano, was providing the entertainment. Things were running smoothly and the guests were thoroughly enjoying the evening when a strange thing happened, prompting the following...

Where's Henry

'Twas a typical Saturday evening,
    and things were right at par.
Many guests sat at the tables,
    and some sat at the bar.

Disco picked up his order
    that Justin had prepared.
David stoked the fireplace.
    Yes, all the work they shared.

John was playing all requests
    as is his normal fashion
Jeanne sipped on her pinot,
    while I had my orange shake passion.

Giulio and Melissa were there
    adding to the party,
Along with new guests from Hartford,
    Anita and Handsome Marty.

Everything was wonderful,
    Nothing to be feared,
When some one asked "Where's Henry?"
    Henry had disappeared.

All eyes looked up for Henry.
    He was nowhere to be found.

John eased up the piano
    when he heard a tapping sound.

It was coming form the backroom.
    The room behind the bar.
The door was closed real tightly,
    not a bit ajar.

As silence fell upon us,
    we heard this mournful plea:
"The darn door will not open.
    Please, help and rescue me!"

Justin tried the key to the door
    where Henry was jailed
The key was of no use.
    The mechanism had failed.

David came to the rescue,
    David is really grand;
David came to the rescue
    with a screwdriver in hand.

He worked it like a surgeon
    and soon everyone cheered
As the bar door did swing open
    and our Henry, he appeared.

All is well that ends well,
    That's how the story goes.
Related to you poetically,
    rather than boring prose!

Sometime around 1950, Jim O'Hearn turned a brick farmhouse on Route 9 into the Century House Restaurant. It became one of the area's most successful dining spots, with excellent cuisine. His sons, Tim and Kevin, joined in and began a series of expansions. Most of these were welcome, except the one I poetically write below.

AN ODE TO TIM AND KEVIN

Last month I went to dinner at the Century House one night.
It was spring with perfect weather, and everything just right.

I had the seafood platter and it suited to a "T".
Along with a glass of wine... Maybe two or three.

The meal, of course, was perfect, but for overeating grief,
I wandered to the bar room for an apertif.
Twas there inflation hit me, right between the eyes,
When I ordered my favorite green drink of ordinary size.

My heart got beating faster, my eyes began to squint.
I had paid two dollars fifty for a rocky crème de menthe.

Now I was really shocked, as I'm sure were many others,
To learn that Tim and Kevin are the Ali Baba brothers.

I got unanimous opinions from every lady and gent.
These boys exceeded the guidelines of our Georgian President.

I'm just an ordinary person, not up on financial games.
But if it were Uncle Jim the barman, I'd feel like Jesse James.

The Century House was rated first, but now it's rated tenth,
For charging twenty bits for a common crème de menthe.

Yet, like MacArthur I'll return, it is still my favorite place.
I love all of the atmosphere and every friendly face.

I just will not be bothered by the brothers and their graft.
I'll simply still enjoy my meal and fill myself with draft.

Sometimes It's Not Rosy

Most marriages are happy and life is but a breeze.
But, one man that I knew, his wife was hard to please.
No way could he please her. His sanity was hard to keep.
Some mornings he'd wake up grouchy, and on some he'd let her sleep.

~~81~~

Many years have gone by since my days had begun,
And now they all total to four score and one.
I had nary a clue that I would get this far,
I must thank Dr. Feeney, my hero, my star.
He checked all my symptoms and fixed all my ills.
Put me on a diet, plus hundreds of pills.
There are a few issues with my life at this junction.
Several parts of my body have diminished function.
Life is still great with love, family, and friends,
I hope for many more years before it all ends.
That I can go on and be reasonably healthy,
And make all of my doctors extremely wealthy.

Down Memory Lane
An Easter Sunday Full House at
The Canaan Congregational Church

The events of this story reach back almost 70 years, somewhere around 1940. The 'big war' was yet to come and the recovery from the Great Depression was well underway. The thriving Village of Canaan boasted a general store, a hotel, a dairy, an ice cream parlor restaurant, a coal and lumberyard, a railroad station, a barber shop, an elementary school, and a service station/repair shop. Times were good!

I confess that the following recollections are of my pre-teen years, way back then, but my memories are strong and vivid of that happy and carefree time of my life. To give further credence to my narrative and to my identity: I was native born and a Canaan resident 'til my family moved when I was thirteen; I am the son of Hazel Steuerwald Jevons, the grandson of Henry and Anna Finch Steuerwald, the nephew of Justice Winthrop and Hilda Foss, and the cousin of Marcia Jensen. All I have mentioned were, or are, members of the Canaan Congregational Church.

This memorable Easter Sunday would not have occurred had it not been for one very special man. His name is Walter Gross. Walter was what might now be described as a "born again" Christian. He was a graduate engineer and family man, who, in his own words, lived a hard and sinful life. He often stated that he had been chased by the devil all across the country. After seeing the light, Walter

Gross became a soapbox missionary; a street corner fire and brimstone preacher in the bowels of New York City. Knowing Walter, I'm sure that many souls were saved.

Entering his "golden" years, Walter left the Big Apple and settled in our little Village of Canaan. He quickly became a member of the Congregational Church and devoted his remaining years to serving the congregation as a deacon and a friend. His home became a meeting place for both youth and adult activities. His car provided transportation to and from church activities for anyone in need. Rides back home often included an ice cream cone from Mayers Red Inn, and his dining room table was always covered with sweet treats. Walter brought a new spirit to the congregation and inspired us all.

Walter's biggest and most noteworthy inspiration took place on the Easter Sunday of my story. The pastor, Reverend Dr. Bartley, became ill and unable to conduct the Easter service on this most holy day. The task fell to Walter Gross.

On most Sundays the church attendance was sparse, and occasionally there were more people in the choir than in the pews. However, the Christmas and Easter services found the congregation filling the seats. So it was on this Easter, when Walter Gross stepped up to the pulpit. He paused for a moment and gazed over the filled pews before him. Walter then looked down at his prepared sermon, and then up to fix his eyes on the congregation. There was noticeable silence as he tossed his sermon to the side. He again looked up at all of us in attendance and then went into the most passionate fire-and-brimstone dialogue that the Good Lord, and the good people of Canaan, had ever heard.

His words were about good and evil, about duty and faith, about sin, about love of God and fellow man, and obligation to church and community... And how it was all related to salvation. He pointed his finger and called out names. There was plenty of blame, and a fair amount of shame. The men bowed their heads, some ladies gasped, and we youngsters squirmed in our britches. The passion of Walter Gross was strong and loud.

It was said that on that Sunday the waters of Queechy rippled, that his echo roared through the tunnel all the way to State Line!

The chairs on Berry's Hotel veranda rocked, and his words roared down the valley like a B&A freight train. Myself, I believe that God smiled and the angels sang. It was an Easter Sunday service never to be forgotten and, in the short term, it wasn't.

On the following Sunday, the church was again full (I would love to be able to report that this continued Sunday after Sunday). Rev. Dr. Bartley made a quick recovery and returned to his place at the pulpit. Walter Gross returned to his role as deacon and friend. The parishioners, bound by human nature, returned to their normal habits. All good people.

It was these good people, and those that have followed, who sustained this church and maintained it as a beacon of faith and a landmark in this wonderful village. So many of the buildings and businesses which were the lifeblood of the Canaan of my childhood, are gone. But the Congregational Church is still the haven of faith and the social center of the community.

My desire to write this story at Easter time was to honor the memory of Walter Gross, Rev. Dr. Bartley, and those good people of

Canaan of that time. I hope it will tweak a memory of that Easter for those congregants still here, and entertain those who have joined us since.

As Dickens wrote "...God bless us, everyone!"

Note: I want to thank Bill and Betsy Bither for sharing their memories and helping me refresh mine.

The Canaan Congregational Church
Artist — Denise Fitzgerald

Pinot ('peeno') Wines

One time beers and whiskies were the choice of libation,
But now fine wines are sweeping the nation.

The reds and the whites and the blushes are glowing.
Yes, the consumption of wine is growing and growing.

There are sauvignons, merlots and cabernets,
With chiantis and rieslings and chardonnays.

Newer on the market from the hillside vines,
Are several new types of Pinot wines.

Pinot Grigio, Pinot Blanco and, of course, Pinot Noir,
Now new on the shelves and the best by far.

For oldsters with problems of incontinence galore.
Is a great new choice, it is called Pinot More!

"The summer place to be," is said of Saratoga Springs, N.Y. The country's oldest race track operates from mid-July till the end of August featuring the world's finest thoroughbreds. Saratoga Polo is, also in operation during that period, playing matches three evenings every week. I enjoy attending these matches and have written a few poems about my experiences.

Tony Coppola has spent almost his entire life in and around polo. He has been a player, an announcer and a club manager. He also owns a business called the Tackeria, which is located on the grounds of the Palm Beach Polo Club. It handles all of the necessary equipment and gear that goes with the sport of polo. Portable units follow the teams to clubs throughout the land, including Saratoga. A few years ago, Tony was inducted into the Polo Hall of Fame in Wellington, Florida. His friends in Saratoga held an evening Gala in his honor. John Walsh of America's Most Wanted was the Master of Ceremonies. It was a combination testimonial and roast. I wrote this poem for the occasion.

Tony Cappola
A Polo Hall of Fame Name

There is no doubt why he made the Hall of Fame,
He's involved in all aspects of the game.
A player, a trainer, and a horseman supreme.
Of the polo crop, Tony is truly the cream.

Around the country, from Florida and back,
His Tackaria provided the players with tack.
He rode the ponies, and mucked the stalls.
He supplied the mallets, and had lots of balls.
Took care of the fields. Kept them level and clear.
And was most outstanding as a divot-teer.
Tony managed the clubs, had them running smooth.
In hippie talk, he was in the groove.

www.tomsullivanphoto.com

www.tomsullivanphoto.com

He played intensely, with passion and verve.
Charged into each play with all kinds of nerve.
The proof of all this was quite often found
With his horse standing there, and him on the ground.

He'll put on the stripes and he'll referee,
And do a good job as one of the three.
But a concern of some players I will relate:
As a player, he still tries to officiate.
Then up into the booth, behind the mike,
He'll call a match that all will like.
His announcing helps make a colorful day,
Because Tony, yes always, has something to say.

Sometimes he is missing. Sort of off on a trip.
Out there somewhere, replacing a hip.

A toast to his honor. That is why we are here.
To all give our Tony a hooray and a cheer!

Now being inducted into the Hall of Fame,
I believe requires a slight change of name.
Drop one p, and an a, then just add an o.
Our Tony now is Mister Co-polo.

The Hole Truth

Our bodies have many openings.
Each has a proper role.
Another word for opening,
It is simply called a hole.

In the head are ears and eye sockets,
Along with throat and mouth.
Other holes can be found
when you are heading south.
Down below the waist line,
More openings in this spectrum.
In the area where you sit down
Are the vagina and the rectum.

dermatolog**ist**   *pulmonolog**ist***   *gastrolog**ist***

urolog**ist**   gynocolog**ist**

*proctolog**ist***   audiolog**ist**   *opthamalog**ist***   orthodont**ist**

Another of great importance,
And very serious in fact,
There's a tiny tube-like channel
Called the urinary tract.

We're covered with skin all over.
We have millions and millions more,
Each of these tiny little holes
Is simply called a pore

There is a doctor for every hole,
'tis a very impressive list.
The title of each physician
Ends with the suffix 'ist'.

These doctor ists are specialists
Within their chosen field.
They will strive to fix your problem,
As soon as it's revealed.

Should the malady be elusive,
As sometimes it takes its toll.
They'll send you to a surgeon,
And he'll make another hole!

In the world of fashion, styles are continually changing. This is a smart business plan, and volumes of new duds are sold because people wish to stay in style. Somehow this hit the basketball world, and tops went to short sleeves and the pants got longer.

A Short Poem

Years ago, when I played in basketball sports,
The uniform consisted of a shirt with shorts.
Now, new in the age of the baby boomers,
The shorts are replaced with lady-like bloomers.
They are loose on the legs, flaring at the knees,
Like clothes on the line, swaying in the breeze.

Playing on defense was once dull and drab,
But now the defender has something to grab.
The refs rarely see how these players are toying,
Disrupting the offense,
    Now that's really annoying.
The answer is short shorts with lots of leg skin.
That is the team that surely will win.
The refs can zoom in on picks, screens, and ball
A better game for the players and fans, one and all.

Irish Gourmet Dining

He was slightly obese and couldn't get thinner,
Being invited to an Irish seven course dinner.

His host, who was gracious and full of good cheer,
Sat him down to a potato and a six-pack of beer.

Miss-Understanding

He confessed to his pretty blond wife
That he was having an affair.
She looked quizzically at him,
With a somewhat empty stare.
All of sudden her eyes lit up,
And then she smiled with glee,
As she asked her startled husband
Who the caterer would be?

What Was the Reason

They had their fortieth anniversary celebration.
Soon after they announced a separation.
It was not infidelity, or for a lack of wealth.
She said, "Frankly, it was a matter of health."
A serious problem, not at all a whim.
"I just got awfully, awfully sick of him!"

Not So Hot

Heaven's Garden Cemetery, in a town called Trent,
Had a crematorium where cadavers were sent.

After a cremation, the ashes they'd return
To the family and loved ones, in an appropriate urn.

To be buried, or kept, or sometimes scattered;
Family choice, that is all that mattered.

Now times have dictated a change for this scene.
The Garden owners decided to go eco-green,
And reduce fossil fuels among other channels,
They covered the roof with solar panels.

The lights worked fine and the heat was to please,
But the furnace ran short by several degrees.

Which brings the fact that I hate to approach:
They could no longer cremate, they only could poach!

A few years back, hurricane Katrina hit the gulf coast, severely flooding the region. The city of New Orleans, with areas below sea level, suffered severe flooding. Devastation was rampant. Funds that were supposed to have strengthened the levees had been spent elsewhere, and warnings to evacuate were ignored. Great suffering ensued. However, with topography below sea level, nothing could have prevented the devastation. Before any rebuilding, I offered this suggestion:

New Orleans - The Big Easy Isn't

The people that planned it must have traits like Satan, the devil,
To build such a large city way down and below the sea level.
Above the Ninth Ward and Parish is a gulf, a lake, and a river,
Enough to make any sensible one shake their head and shiver.
One has to know and realize, when he is filling his cup,
That liquids flow only down. Liquids never flow up.
The hurricane surge did come and gave the waters a hefty shove,
Cascading down into the city from all three bodies above.
The pumps, they were to fail, that was a foregone conclusion,
When billions and billions of gallons made the great intrusion.
We must rebuild the Big Easy, somehow, one way or another.
Let us all seek out the opinions of every dear sister and brother.
Do we do it where it was before, or build in some other place?
To work to rebuild it as it is would be a terrible disgrace.
There are purple mountain majesties in many another state
To send rail cars full of fill. Now wouldn't that be great?
Tons and tons of gravel to help fill that woeful hole.
And then rebuild that city, right there atop that bowl.
It would rise above so majestic, way up there and higher.
Proud as it always was before, and definitely much drier!

The Green Grass Grows

I have this bothering question.
A question I'm eager to share.
Lawns with those **"Keep Off the Grass"** signs,
How in heck are they placed out there?

A ladies tournament was featured during the summer season at the Saratoga Polo Club. Female players came from all over. The matches were exciting and very well played. There were outstanding performances by both players and ponies. Only one small problem arose which is related in poetic form below.

The Ladies Play Polo

The Ladies played polo on the Skidmore field.
Very good players, that was quickly revealed.

There was one slight problem confusing the view,
Both teams' shirts had the same tint and hue.

A shot was taken, the flag raised with a roar.
But which team was it making the score?

Kids on a playground pick teams for a game,
pressed in street clothes, they all look the same.

Being ingenious, they came up with a plan,
So every teammate knew who was his man.

I suggest for the ladies, so we know who wins,
Next time, like the kids did, play shirts and skins!!!

BOTHERSOME

There was this lovely sheepdog
and I must tell you, please,
He was always bothered by moths
and never bothered by fleas

S.C

When I was young and feeling great,
I measured up to five feet eight.
Growing older, it is not a surprise,
A person begins to diminish in size.
I must admit that it's got me thinking,
That, I myself, am doing some shrinking.
I still feel good and I get my kicks
But, at eighty-two, I'm now five foot six.

To live to two hundred, I'd like to do,
But, by then, I'd be only three foot two!

Cat Lesson Learned

Tabby was a handsome cat
And he was proud and strong.
Thinking he was very smart
And could do nothing wrong.

One day he jumped atop the stove.
The stove was very hot.
Thus Tabby burned his buttocks
When squatting down he sot.

This cat has learned his lesson,
The stove top is out of bounds.
Yes, this he will remember
When walking on his rounds.

Now his tender little backside
Is there for all to see.
We have this feline story
About a cat-ass-trophe.

S.C.

Some of the poems I wrote about the Trapp Family Resort were designed to go into their suggestion box. The poem about removing some trees to obtain a view of the mountains from the dining room was accepted. The trees were removed and there is now a magnificent view. This poem is about adding an executive type golf course. Maybe someday, stay tuned.

PLEASURE AND NATURE - MY VACATION HOME

My vacation days, I want to spend
Where pleasure and nature are a perfect blend.
What place is this? Ask if you will.
It's in Stowe, Vermont, up on Trapp Hill.
The lodge sits there, with the forest behind,
Meadows and pastures, you also will find.
Timeshares and Villas spread out on the scene,
Surrounded by trees and patches of green.
Once settled in, amid this nature and beauty,
Enjoy and relax, it's your only duty.
Cross-country ski trails, miles to your liking,
With seasonal uses for hiking and biking.
If it's the playing of tennis of which you are fond,
The courts are there, just below the pond.
There are two fine pools for swimming fun,
Surrounded by chairs to soak up some sun.
During inclement weather, you can easily enter
The new, multi-activity fitness center.
Take a walk to the Chapel or The Sugar House.
Go it solo or bring family and spouse.
With turkeys and deer and others of God's creatures,
More of the nature that Trapp Hill features.
Plus the Scottish Highlanders always amaze,
As they roam the pastures and quietly graze.
Next, a plan for the future, added and amended,
For the use of God's earth the way He intended:
Build a small golf course for sport and fun

With only nine holes, about a par thirty-one.
To fill the off-season with more guests and action,
And to bring to Trapp Hill another attraction.
Then a sensible layout, well-planned and true,
With trees, rolling fairways, and a pond or two.
The fairways in winter could possibly be
Several more meters to cross-country ski.
An earth-friendly golf course, another sensation,
At Trapp Family Lodge, a great destination.

History — Two Centuries Apart

When we were in school we all learned about Paul Revere and his warnings of the British invasion of Boston. He used lanterns on the bell tower of the Old North church. Recently, Sheryl Crow, a songstress living in the fantasy world of Hollywood, issued a suggestion for saving our trees. Her idea was to use less toilet paper by cutting down on the number of squares.

Revere (with lanterns)-   "One if by land,
                                          Two if by sea."
Crow (with tissue squares)- "Two if you poop,
                                          One if you pee."

~~83~~

I am feeling fine except for my neurotrophic legs.
A result of diet choices and far too many kegs.
Along with the arthritis, my legs have lost some talents;
Like the ability to run, and most important, balance.
Otherwise, I'm fine, thanks to God and medical science,
With all the vital organs still working in compliance.
Of course, I am most thankful for yet another year,
To enjoy all those around me, my heart is full of cheer.
Now I've started hoping for at least one year more,
So I can write another poem when I reach eighty-four.

Obama's Promises

I promise you this one thing
That will happen nevermore.
No legislation will be conducted
Behind that old closed door.

All negotiations will be open,
That is my promised plan,
And citizens can watch it all
On TV cameras, with C-SPAN.

Together the sides will banter
For all the world to see.
My office will not be secret,
Yes, this I promise thee.

One year after he was elected,
He has failed to keep his vow.
Honest reporters and politicos
Are starting to question how

He could break so many promises
As such a short time flies?
I submit they were not promises
But devious political lies.

It's the game plan of the liberals
To push their agenda along.
If Mr. Obama was made of wood,
His nose would be one mile long!

The laughable Charles Schumer, the Senator from New York, loves to jump in front of the TV cameras. He craves publicity and has a tendency to say whatever he thinks his listeners want to hear. He will go both ways on any issue. One example is when he called for tighter airline security only a few days after he said nasty things about a flight attendant who insisted he shut down his cell phone prior to take-off.

I had a dream about the Senator one night during the Federal Government stimulus debates. On awakening, I decided to relate my dream. It follows.

A Stimulus Parody - Pardon Me

There are several billion dollars for urban canals in the newly passed, so-called stimulus plan. Out of curiosity, I called the Senate office building in Washington, D.C., and was connected with the office of my state senator, Chuck Schumer.

"Hello, Senator Schumer's office."

"Hi, my name is Gordon and I have a question for the Senator." "You're in luck, Mr. Gordon. The Senator is right here."

"Wow!"

"Chuck Schumer here. Are you Gordon?"

"Yes, sir. And I have a question."

"I'll be happy to answer it, Gordon, just as soon as I get my TV crew and cameras in place. (Pause) Okay, we are ready. What is the question?"

"What are those Urban Canals in that stimulus bill and did you read the bill?"

"No, I didn't have time to read the bill due to all my TV appearances, but I can tell you all about Urban Canals."

"Please do, sir."

"Well, let me tell you. Those canals are going to crate millions of jobs and help counter the effects of Global Warming. They will be green and help clean the air. The will also boost tourism throughout the land and provide us with a useful byproduct. And most of all, the American people have said they want these canals."

"Amazing! Tell me about the creation of those jobs."

"We are going to need engineers to design the canals and manufacturers to make the construction equipment. There will be thousands of laborers to excavate, and thousands of pavers for the walls and canal floor. Then, thousands more will be needed to build the gondolas, and foresters to cut the propelling poles. Colleges will train the gondoliers and navigators. That is what I call job creation!"

"Glory-owski! And, how do the canals help with the effect of global warming?"

"Gordon, when those arctic ice caps melt and the oceans rise up twenty feet, we'll just push that water into all those canals and keep the sea levels where they are."

"Gee whiz and wow again!"

"Also, there will be no engines or motors to pollute the air. Pole pushing will propel the gondolas. Urban transportation will be on the canals. No more buses, cars, taxis, trains, trucks, bicycles, or rickshaws in urban America to create pollution."

"Hot darn! Did I hear you mention a tourist attraction?"

"I'm sure you heard of Venice in Italy, that famous magic town? Where the streets are shining rivers and the boats glide up and down. Millions visit that city every year."

"Jumping geniuses! Oh, you mentioned a byproduct?"

"This could be the best part, Gordon. We are going to take all of the excavated material and ship it to New Orleans to fill in that hole of a ninth ward and raise it above sea level so that it will never flood again!"

"Marvy marvelous! And I would guess that the best part of this plan is that the American people really want it."

"To be honest, Gordon, I'm not sure about that. We liberals and our National Corrupt Media always use that phrase to help us get what we want."

"Now we know!"

"Thank you, Gordon. I hope this was helpful to you. Please call again."

"God Bless America."

The Peef Plant

Native to the wetlands and ponds of the Von Trapp Family Resort property in Northern Vermont, there grows a form of vegetation with greenish-yellow fan shaped leaves. This is commonly known as the Peef Plant. In the autumn of the year, the leaves of the Peef Plant turn in color to a blazing red.

The frogs living in the ponds and wet lands of the area were, somehow, enhanced by the bright red leaves and spent hours jumping back and forth over the leaf tops.

This Amphibian activity, most likely, is where the term "leap frog" originated.

Also, it is most interesting to note, that these <u>Peef leapers</u> were present here in Vermont, long before the coming of the annual bus loads of <u>leaf peepers</u>.

Copied from Encyclopedia Vermont 2005 Edition

Matt Graves, a good friend, covered the horse racing news for the Albany Times Union. His work was well received and he earned several national honors. Matt worked with Tim Wilken, another good sports reporter. Matt is well known for his quick wit and sense of humor. When in the company of friends, verbal quips often fly in both directions. Tim, however, is of a more serious nature. During the winter season each was assigned to cover a local team. The team results gave me inspiration for this poem. Matt enjoyed the humor. Tim didn't.

A few years back, in order to lower expenses,
The editorial staff lost their common senses.
Horse racing coverage was the task that was Matt's
He was then assigned hockey, our own River Rats.
Go back to that time, make note of the date,
When the Rats started losing at a terrible rate.
This silly group of Ed's, with no thought but with whim,
Gave Siena basketball to the writer named Tim.

The Saints they did play and had losses galore,
The fans started crying and Coach Rob was no more.
It is so easy to fathom, just look at the stats,
Tim did to the Saints what Matt did to the Rats.

The Hereafter

Aging, I think of hereafter.
It comes with a bit of laughter.

I go somewhere to get something and
Wonder what I'm here after.

In 2008, Chris Matthews, a national television commentator, stated that when he listened to Barack Obama speak, he felt a tingle or thrill running up and down his leg. WOW... That is some real form of idolization!

Chris Matthews is a liberal who has no common sense,
And he hates all conservatives, both ladies and the gents.
He makes outrageous statements, he's not concerned with truth.
Yet, he believes the fairy that left a penny for his tooth.
As a serious commentator, he is laughable at best,
Which leads me to attempt this little poetic jest.

When Chris felt that thrilling tingle, I suggest by chance,
'Twas simply urination running down his pants!

Did you ever have a song and lyrics repeating over and over in your mind? The following poem is the result of just that. A wonderfully talented vocal artist, Colleen Pratt, with a world class voice, recorded the jazz classic "I Thought About You". It was written by Jimmy VanHuesen and Johnny Mercer, and performed by such greats as Frank Sinatra and Ella Fitzgerald. Colleen's version was the one in my head. One night, while staying in a hotel in Salem, I jotted down the words over and over again. I dedicate it to all who, in their lifetime, think about that special love.

Just after midnight as the day started new,
I opened my eyes and I thought about you.
I woke up again, just before two,
Pictured your beauty and I thought about you.
The sun in the morning sparkled the dew,
I looked out the window and thought about you.
With a hearty breakfast, before I started to chew,
I looked at my scrambles and I thought about you.
Then a drive up the coast and the ocean so blue,
With shimmering white caps and I thought about you.
Arriving at the Wentworth, standing tall and true,
I looked at that structure and thought about you.
The beautiful wait girls, one with a tattoo,
Served me my luncheon and I thought about you.
My birthday dessert, before the candle I blew,
I made me a wish and I wished to have you.
Heading back down to Salem, how the miles they flew,
With each bump and each curve, I thought about you.
After dinner and drinks, I had quite a few,
I felt really happy and I thought about you.
Climbing into my bed, after dropping each shoe,
Ready for dreaming, yes, to dream about you.

In 2008, Barack Obama was elected President of the United States, and was sworn into office in January of 2009. Relatively unknown, prior to taking office, his words, actions, and policies soon awakened a sleeping love-of-country majority. Constitutional conservatives arose. The Tea Party movement was born. And, in 2010, conservatives swept in and took control of Congress. In the extremely liberal state of Massachusetts, Scott

Brown, a republican, was elected into the U.S. Senate. All of this prompted the following:

The New Paul Revere

When his presidential campaign was in trouble and failin'
John McCain gave to us marvelous Sarah Palin.

When Mr. Obama was taking our constitution down,
The people of the Bay State gave us Mr. Scott Brown.

He inspired the electorate and they gave him their vote.
He won against all odds, and the nation took note.

No longer need we cower. No longer need we fear.
Scott Brown awoke the country, like a new Paul Revere.

With the likes of Scott and Sarah we now do have a choice.
Repeat the Bay State in November and the world will rejoice.

The constitution will be saved. The bells of freedom will ring.
When people are informed, democracy is a wonderful thing.

Of the many things to which the Trapp Family Resort is dedicated, one is nature. Therefore, only the main arterial leading to the Lodge is paved. All other roads and the parking areas are natural - dirt! Moving about on these roads, at times, can be an adventure,

Traveling the Von Trapp Roads - - Pot-HOLE- Luck

Going to the timeshare from the pavement to the gravel,
becomes a most serious and interesting travel.

Slowly you zig to the left and zag to the right,
ducking and dodging - a most curious sight.

The potholes grow bigger and even more numerous
and the balcony watchers think it quite humorous.

Try going past the Deli to the Laundry Exchange.
To call that a driveway is really real strange.

There are moguls and dips and numerous holes,
that are definitely a test for guest owner souls.

Yes, the roads are in serious need of refinement,
Before all of our cars have lost their alignment!

Eye Tricks

Sometimes your eyes will play tricks on you,
I've come to that conclusion.

One day I viewed a large mirage, but
'Twas only an optical illusion!

Pain Relief

This pretty blonde miss, whose looks were exquisite,
Made a trip to her doctor, a most painful visit.

He asked of her problem and why she had came.
She told him she ached, her whole entire frame.

He instructed, "Stretch out on the table over there,
And use your finger to show me just where.

She pushed her finger to her head right through her hair,
And let out a yell that anyone would scare.

Then the finger went down onto her shoulder,
While the screams of pain got bolder and bolder.

She then touched her torso, just above the belt.
It was so obvious, the great pain that she felt.

The same thing happened when she prodded her leg,
Relief from the doctor she frantically did beg.

"Oh, doctor," she asked, "How long will this pain linger?"
"As soon," he replied, "As I can set your broken finger."

Shortly into his second term, President William Jefferson Clinton was faced with an embarrassing scandal. He had engaged in oral sexual activity with a young intern in the Oval Office. When questioned by the proper authorities, he did a great deal of ducking, dodging, and verbal gymnastics; much of his testimony was hilarious. However, the evidence was overwhelming and in the end he was impeached, but not removed from office --which was another disgrace. Below is a poem about some of his verbal antics.

A member of the Grand Jury: "Mr. President, my question is - Were you ever alone with Miss Lewinsky?"

It Depends Upon the Meaning of the Word Is

Mr. Clinton's reply:

The question itself has a contentious tone.
First, I must know what you mean by **alone**
And, as a college grad and a Rhodes scholar wiz,
I have a problem whether it's **is, is** or **is**?
Before I can give you a strong firm never,
You need to explain, is it **ever** or **ever**?
Then after we agree to which one of the **is is**,
Can we then define, is it **Ms., Miss,** or **Mrs.**
Sheepishly, I request and hope you will do.
Please spell, so I'll know, if it is **you** or **ewe**
Were I understand, and **with** is quite easy.
But, if I answer with yes, you'll know I am sleazy.
So, I must be evasive, appearing uncouth.
Dooming myself if I present you with truth.
Thus, leave your question, as of now, in abatement,
And, I'll revert you right back to my earlier statement!

Dan Rather, once a respected and trusted television journalist, messed up and was fired by his long-time employer, CBS. Over the years, Dan developed strong left-leaning tendencies and lost all fairness in his reporting. He used falsified military documents to hinder the election of George W. Bush for a second presidential term. Despite the fact several sources proved the documents to be phony, Dan insisted they were true and continued to stand by his story. All of this prompted me to further investigate the matter. I interviewed several famous people who supported Mr. Rather's questionable reporting.

He told me Dan was right, as I sat there at his table
That was renowned Mr. Aesop - master of The Fable

"If you really think he's wrong, you are a true buffoon"
This was related to me by the famous Man in the Moon

"I was there!   It's true and that's how it goes!"
Yes, you can be sure, because 'the Shadow knows

"When people doubt our Dan, it becomes to me real scary"
I gleaned this fact from my grandson's very own Tooth Fairy

And with the forensic accuracy of famed dear Doctor Baden,
Mister Rather was affirmed by the terrorist Bin Laden

Another confirmation from one that we all know,
Our beloved wooden puppet - the liar, Pinocchio

Plus one who knows who's good - it came without pause,
"Danny got it right-"   This came from Santa Claus

"For those who are contrary, we wish them all the Pox!"
This came from huge Paul Bunyon and his famous Big Blue Ox

Now all these phony experts are of the phony kind,
Just like the phony story that Dan made up in his mind

The facts, they cannot be denied - that is so easy to see,
How Rather lost completely his credibility

Let us now forget this issue - so designed to try us,
Agreeing Dan was done-in by his very own hateful bias

Many children have problems swallowing pills or are reluctant to try. One pharmaceutical company created vitamin pills based on the animated TV comedy of pre-historic characters called the Flintstones. The vitamin packed pills were tasty, colorful, and in the shape of the featured characters. The youngsters seemed to enjoy them and received their daily dose of supplemental vitamins.

Not Hard To Swallow

I tried the Flintstone vitamins.
They were tasty like a treat.

I didn't feel much healthier,
But I could stop the car with my feet!

A Hairy Hare Experience

A man was out driving, one bright sunny day,
Happily cruising on the old state highway.
When suddenly on the road, a rabbit appeared.
To avoid the bunny he swerved and veered.
Alas, all his efforts were a bit too late,
And that tiny hare suffered a terrible fate.

Feeling sad he pulled over in the breakdown lane,
Walked back to the rabbit, his heart filled with pain.
Upset he was, that his maneuver did fail.
Lifted that bunny and sat down by the rail.

A lady out driving saw this curious sight,
Pulled off and stopped, to help if she might.
He related to her how the event did take place.
She returned to her car, a smile on her face.

She came back from her car with an aerosol can,
And sprayed that poor hare being held by the man.

That bunny jumped up and did hop after hop,
Then turned and waved, after once he did stop.
He kept hopping and waving until out of view.
It is a true story I'm relating to you.

Extremely elated this most curious man,
Questioned the lady of her miracle can.
She displayed the can with not one word to say.
Pointed to the title, it read Hair Spray
Then under the title, a line printed there,
"This restores life to newly dead hair."
The delighted man with gratitude did rave
When he read the next line: "Adds permanent wave!"

A few years ago, Dr. William Feeney, my primary care physician, prescribed a new medication to help control my diabetes. Byetta, the medication, is contained in a needle pen and is injected twice daily. The instructions were to keep it under refrigeration when not in use. This poem is written from an actual experience.

A Medication Mix-Up

Early in the morning, after nighttime slumber,
I must medicate, to control my sugar number.
I'm dosing with Byetta. A brand new med that's hot,
And applied quite neatly, with a tiny needle shot.

Doctor Feeney did prescribe it, this newer healthy plan.
He is a very good doctor, as well as a very good man.
His efforts have made my health improve.
I'm feeling just fine and I'm in the groove.

In modern times, when your meds run low,
Back to your doctor, you need not go.
A phone plea to his office, nothing else, that's all.
They, in turn, give the drugstore a call.

I went into the store, to the pharmacy in back,
Gave the clerk my name and she went to the rack.
"Now hold on a minute!" I spoke loud and quite bold
"That medication needs to be kept in the cold."

In the phone communication
there was some how a mistake.
It was the drug Viagra that
was packaged for me to take!

I'll remember that day
just as long as I live.
I needed an injection to take.
Not one to give.

A quick call back to the doctor and they made everything right.
Now I, and all others, can sleep well at night

GRANDPA STEUERWALD HAD A QUESTION

Grandpa repaired an axle for Max Stall, his Canaan friend,
Who lived up o'er the hill and down around the bend.

Max, a cabinetmaker, had a greater self-intention.
He wanted to be famous for an outstanding invention.

In spare time he would tinker and toil to get it done.
A fascinating product that would astonish everyone.

When Grandpa arrived with the axle,
        Max was in his shop,
Working on an invention.
        He didn't want to stop.

"Max what are you making?
        Your axle I did bring."
"It's a super solvent, Henry.
        It will dissolve anything!"

Grandpa thought it over a
        moment with a twisted grin.
Then inquired of his friend,
        "What will you keep it in?"

Eliot Spitzer, the former state attorney general, was elected governor of New York. He was extremely arrogant and described himself as a steamroller who would destroy his opponents. His short tenure and downfall came when a New York City newspaper exposed his frequent use of an expensive call girl from New York that he patronized in Washington D.C. The call girl agency had him listed as client number nine.

ELIOT BY THE NUMBERS

He promised to change New York- a most prestigious run
Right after inauguration, it was going to start day ONE

He had a lust for power and a plan he had to do
He controlled the governor's office and the assembly made that TWO

He crazed to gain the senate and said "it had to be"
Complete control of New York State, for then he'd have all THREE

With the state police as his ally, he made another score
Along with Darren Dopp, he had a team of FOUR

The Times Union then joined in- my goodness, sakes alive!
Now the devious team of Spitzer was up to number FIVE

Down the road much later, after many dirty tricks
District attorney Soares got honest with investigation number SIX

How many times did Spitzer use the hooker?
With lust, desire and endeavon
Spending many thousands- t'was somewhere around SEVEN

Along with all his nasties, we add in "Troopergate"
Bringing Spitzer's dirty deeds up to number EIGHT

What caused his resignation and brought the "end of the line"
Was when The Post newspaper exposed him as Client Number NINE

Wallstreet started cheering, someone should write a song
Good-bye to Mr. Spitzer, the arrogance is gone

In 2009 the New York State Senate came to a standstill when two downstate democrat senators switched over to the republican side and changed the balance of power. Immediately, before any business could be conducted, Neil Breslin gaveled the session to adjournment without the mandatory motion, second, and approval. He ordered the lights out and the locking of all doors and records. It was a complete republican lockout. Pouting and quarreling, in very serious economic and financial times, no state business was conducted for weeks.

BLAME THIS MESS ON BRESLIN

The senate was running smoothly until that fateful hour,
When two democrats crossed over, changing who had the power.

Neil Breslin had the gavel, this everyone should note,
And he quickly closed the session without a legal vote.

They acted like spoiled children, doing nothing right,
And locked up all the doors, and turned off every light.

They could have avoided chaos and stayed and worked things out,
Acting like grown-up leaders and not like kids that pout.

Nothing is getting done, as they say, "that's all she wrote,"
Because Breslin failed to honor a perfectly legal vote.

You shouldn't be disappointed, what else did you expect,
My grandpa always told me, "you get what you elect".

Creation

After creating the earth, and the animal creatures,
God decided a human should be one of the features.
Thus, God continued his universal plan.
In his very own image, he created a man.
A pure and handsome fellow --Adam was his name,
The first to inhabit this earth, truly was his fame.

There in the Garden of Eden, a paradise sublime,
Is where Adam roamed alone, and where he spent his time.

One day God asked of Adam, "Is there anything else you need?"
Adam replied, "A companion would be very nice, indeed."
God gazed down upon Adam and then he did inquire,
"What kind of companion is it, that you so desire?"
Adam, a careful thinker, this proposal he did render,
"How about a human of the opposite gender?"
"A female of beauty and brains would be completely grand,
Who would always obey, never argue and follow my command.

God heard the request and knew that the order was tall.
Yet, he quickly replied, there was no pause or no stall.
"A woman that is perfect. Adam, there is no need to beg
But, my son, that will cost you all of an arm and a leg."
Adam paused and then slowly, in a voice most pensive and glib,
Said, "Please tell me, my Lord, what can I get for a rib?"

The Better Bettor

Some people go to the racetrack just to watch the ponies run.
Many will make wagers to win some cash and have some fun.
The most serious of players who have horse racing smarts,
Will weigh all of the factors and study all the charts.
Past performances and breeding are among items figured in.
Plus checking the competition, can this horse really win?
The condition of the surface, the gambler needs to know.
Is the racetrack listed fast, or is it muddy or only slow?
The equipment on the steed is important to these thinkers.
Is he wearing special shoes, or a shadow roll or blinkers?
They all are handicappers and are students of the game.
Well known at all the ovals, they share an amount of fame.

Then, there are those strange methods of some people that I know,
To select their horse of choice to win, or place, or show.
They like that horse's name, or the number on his back,
Or, the way he holds his head, while walking to the track.
Some wager on the color like black, brown, roan or gray.
And others play the jockey, Could this be his lucky day?
Some bet a winning trainer. Todd Pletcher's of that renown.
Except on major races. Like those of the Triple Crown.

In conclusion, by this survey,
    betting schemes are somewhat treacherous.
And, betting solely on the trainer,
    that indeed, is really Pletcherous!

For almost 100 years, the capitol city of Albany, New York, and its surrounding county have been under the control of the Democrat Party. Most of the townships in that county are also controlled by the Democrats. One glaring example of the opposite is the town of Colonie, which has been under Republican leadership for much of the last 100 years. Every two years in the election cycle, the Democrats try desperately to unseat the Republicans. I begged the following questions.

I ask if it's the taxes. Is that the reason you found?
"No, it's not the taxes. They are the lowest around."
Are the roads and streets a problem and make you feel not proud?"
"Oh no," they say, "They're wide and clean, well-paved and quickly plowed."
Is it our fire protection and that you live in fear?
"Not at all," they answer, "Our men are trained and have the latest gear."
Could it be our many parks, are they not to your liking?
"No, the parks are simply grand for swimming, sports, and hiking."
Then it must be the police department. You're not safe and live in fear?
"Gosh, no," they answer. "We have the lowest crime rate every single year."
Our Sanford Public Library, is that the cause of your concern?
"Well, no, it's a great place to visit, read, research, and learn."
Then is it our schools? You think they are not great?
"Oh, yes, we do, they are the very best in all the state!"
Pray tell me then, where the Republicans are wrong.
"They're not! It's just that they've been in charge too long."
I stand there in amazement. View them with scorn and pity.
'Cause they don't feel that way about Albany County and City.

There was a recent media flap over a college co-ed demanding free birth control for her sexual activities. It became a big verbal battle between liberals and religious conservatives. I offered this wonderful, no-cost suggestion that will work without fail.

Two birth control drugs, Proven effective by trial are:
Noassatall   and   Selphadenial

Church Contributions

Many of our rural churches have a very limited cash flow.
Usually needed projects, are handled pay as you go.
That is just the way it was in an upstate little town,
That got a message one Sunday from the Reverend Pastor Brown.

The furnace needed severe repair. This the Pastor noted.
An extra collection was the answer. For this the stewards voted.
So, on the Sunday service, the Pastor who was inventive,
Announced a special collection and added some incentive.

We're accepting your donations all through this corning week
Whoever gives the most will be the winner that we seek.
At next Sundays service, the winner gets three hymns to choose,
To inspire our Holy program, no one will really lose.

Widow Morgan won the honor, with a check of very good size.
Pastor Brown announced the winner and everyone turned their eyes.
He then asked widow Morgan to name the hymns she chose.
She stood up very proudly and slid her glasses up her nose.

Looked the congregation over with a smile and a whim.
Then pointing with her finger said, "I'll take him and him and him!"

While preparing forty-eight hours for an invasive medical examination, I amused myself by writing this poem. Please, feel free to enter the politician of your choice.

A Colonoscopy Moment

The word colonoscopy has only O's for a vowel.
It is a medical exam of one's lower bowel.
A tiny camera is inserted, that is a fact,
To take pictures inside of the elimination tract.
You are kindly sedated for this medical test
To find any condition that must be addressed.
The most un-comforting thing in this physical bout
Is the pre-day procedure to empty you out.
There's no solid food all day, that's without question,
Only liquids and pills to flush your digestion.
That day and through the night, my fortitude was taxed,
But by morning, I was ready, calm and relaxed.
I arrived at the center, empty to the bone.
Another guy was there, I wasn't alone.
We were prepared and made ready to walk the walk.
To pass the time we started to talk.
He praised Obama spouting socialistic views,
A classic puppet of biased liberal media views.
I told him" cancel your test, it will not work a bit."
I knew by his words, he was still full of shit!

In 2010 three men were in the race for the New York State Governorship. I made this poetic observation.

O Governor

The year is 2010 and Election Day is coming.
Interest is high, and the polls and news are humming.
In New York State there will be an interesting race,
Where three men all are running for the Spitzer-Patterson place.

The democrats are backing the son of a favorite son,
Mario Cuomo's boy Andrew has decided he will run.
The man that lost to Hillary, once again, wants to go,
He licked his wounds and is ready. That is Rick Lazio.
Carl Paladino, the businessman, won't take it anymore.
The Tea Party is behind him, they think that he can score.
The democrats are numerous and hold a very strong edge.
But times today are troubling and could help to drive a wedge.
Predictions are precarious, yet one thing I do know:
New York State's next governor, his name will end in O!

I Found the Answer

I started my teaching career at Middleburgh Central School in the Schoharie valley of New York State. To supplement my income, I served as an assistant to the basketball coach. I have many memories of that wonderful experience.

One strange memory that I pondered over the many years came from a game against the high school from Canajoharie. I do remember that they won the game; however, I remember most the energetic cheerleading squad from that Mohawk Valley school. Back in those days a popular cheer was the "Locomotive." When those girls finished with all the letters from Canajoharie, it was one of the longest cheers I ever experienced. I do remember most the individual cheer. Whenever a player went in or out of the game he got a "yeah" and a "rah" and a "yeah, rah". One player in particular was inserted into and taken out of the Canajoharie line up frequently. All game long I heard "Yeah Pilltoochee, Rah Pilltoochie, Yeah, Rah, Pilltoochee." Thinking back over the years, I always wonder was that his last name, or were there two words?

Almost sixty years later I was sitting with my friend, enjoying the music in the lounge of The Trapp Family Lodge in Stowe, Vermont. A very nice couple at the next table engaged me in conversation. They enjoy the Lodge as much as we do and are also frequent guests. We discovered we had many experiences in common. I had graduated from the State College at New Paltz the same year that he graduated from the state school at Oswego. We had gone to different colleges together. I had a son and grandson who also graduated from Oswego. The wife had graduated from the state school at

Geneseo. One of my daughters was a graduate and a granddaughter is now attending Geneseo. The wife also grew up in the Village of Canajoharie and was in school at the time of the beginning of this story. She was able to answer the question that had been bothering me all these many years and confirmed that, indeed, Pilltoochie was two names. There were many other times and places that we have in common with this wonderful couple and I hope to stay in touch and make plans to meet with them again. Until then, just one more time let's hear it:

"Yeah, Bill Tucci! Rah, Bill Tucci! Yeah, Rah, Bill Tucci!"

Electronically Controlled State of the Nation

Wednesday nights speech on the state of the nation
I became aware of this curious revelation.
I dutifully watched and then did behold,
The entire event was electronically controlled.
To insure the President did not appear absurd,
The teleprompters controlled each and every word.
The director, behind the scene was fully engaged,
To make sure the event was most properly staged.
Vice President Biden and the Speaker Pelosi were there,
Behind Barack Obama and each had a chair.
Nancy was given a very special job to do.
And, was told to respond when given her cue.
When Barack made a point deserving some laud,
She was told to stand up and quickly applaud.
The director who was, also, the speech regulator,
Installed in her chair a buzzing vibrator.

To have her act on cue
    a button he would push,
And she would get the signal
    right there on her tush.
After several cues it began
    appearing quite hollow.
Each time she jumped up,
    Joe Biden would follow.
For the future I suggest,
    to be perfectly fair
Add such a device to the
    Vice President's chair.
Alternating the cues let him lead,
    jumping with class,
Each time he feels that
    buzzer under his ass.

I miss Tony Snow. He was a fantastic TV journalist and the White House Press Secretary for George W. Bush. A fine family man, he left this life much too early, a victim of cancer. He is considered to be one of the best Press Secretaries ever. He was a real contrast to the current one, Jay Carney, who is one of the worst. I vented:

One of the highlights of summertime in my youth was when the carnival came to town. The carnival had a country fair-like set up with exciting rides, sideshows, games of chance, and interesting dining delights. There were corn dogs, hoagies, cotton candy, and soda pop. The carnival was in town for a few days up to a week. The carnival workers were called "carneys". Parents informed their youngsters that the carneys were not to be trusted. Carnival time was the only period of the year when homes were locked when no one was home.

The purpose of the carnival was fun and entertainment. The job of the carneys was to separate you from large suns of your money. They relied on illusions and falsehoods to entice you into a sideshow or try a game of chance. The truth was a concept never employed by a carney.

They made their living telling lies and misleading the listener.

Isn't it ironic that we now have a Carney working in the White House? Jay Carney. And, he fits the role of a carney to a T.

Family restaurants and roadside diners feature common grand-mother-type soups that are both hearty and filling. Chicken noodle, vegetable beef, tomato, clam chowder, and split pea are the offerings. To-day, up-scale fine dining establishments offer soups with exotic names and strange ingredients. When this is the case, I often go soupless.

Souper Soups

When I was young and old-fashioned back there,
Soup on a menu, was welcome and standard fare.
They were hearty and tasty. Full of ingredients
Of familiar delights that made common sense.

Some modern day chefs become extremely erotic,
Designing soups with names they think are exotic.
Like the offering last night, I said "Oh my gosh!"
The given name was **Sweet Potato and Butternut Squash**
Some of the others I'll relate, none of them plain:
Pear and Apple Bisque. Cheddar Lager and **Strawberry Champagne,**

Along with **Gorgonzola Mushroom.** I thought "What the heck!"
There was **Tomato Fennell, Gazpacho,** and **Krautmitspeche.**
I tried them all. I am known to take risk.
The **Chilled Mojito, Vichyssoise** and **Parsnip Bisque.**

I miss my **Chicken with Noodle,** and **Veggies with Beef.**
They are tasty and filling, providing hunger relief.
As I intensely continue, my thoughts grow louder,
I miss my **Campbell's Tomato** and a proper **Clam Chowder.**
If it's not a conspiracy, it's a terrible scam;
Doing away with **French Onion** and **Split Pea with Ham.**

91

Thank god for those chefs that are still able and willing
To make grandma-type soups that are tasty and filling.

I have a suggestion for the new culinary type
Make basic soups using some vocabulary hype.
They can be made to sound exotic. From deep down in my wits
Make a *Vegetable Consume with Grass-fed Beef Bits*
I'll explain what I said. Yes, here is the scoop
What I described is just plain *Beef Vegetable Soup*.

Podded Legumes Divided with Pork that is Cured
Is a soup, in reality, that is loved and endured.
Those fancy words for that broth? An outrageous scam
What I just told you was *Split Pea with Ham*.

All you culinary experts, give the diners a choice.
Create two soups each day and all will rejoice
Create familiar phrases that earn praise and extol.
But the proof of the pudding, is what is there in the bowl.

It is time to say good-bye or good night. When I was a very young lad, my parents would take me to an early evening Saturday dance at the Queechy Lake Casino. The evening always ended with the same song. Many, many years later, at my restaurant and lounge, I had the band end the evening with that very same song. It was sung and performed over the years by Rudy Vallee, Guy Lombardo, Ray Noble and many others. The title is Good Night Sweetheart.

> Good Night Sweetheart, till we meet tomorrow
> Good night sweetheart, sleep will banish sorrow
> Tears and parting may make us forlorn
> But with the dawn a new day is born
> So I'll say
> Good night sweetheart, tho' I'm not beside you,
> Good night sweetheart, still my love will guide you,
> Dreams enfold you, In each one I'll hold you.
> Good night sweetheart, good night.

Good night,
Grandpa Gordon